AF268744

Sozo:

What am I Saved From?

Kirkland M. Rite

Printed in the United States of America

First Printing: 2026

Eternal Kingdom International Publishing, LLC

LIBRARY OF CONGRESS

LCCN: 2026940838

ISBN- 978-1-968815-24-0 - Paperback

ISBN- 978-1-968815-23-3 - eBook

ISBN- 978-1-968815-25-7 - Hardcover

A Note from EKI Publishing:

This book is part of a larger Kingdom reading pathway developed through EKI Books. These works are designed to help readers grow from foundational truths into mature Kingdom life, moving from repentance, identity, and inner restoration into transformation, body life, leadership, and deeper revelation. While each book may be read on its own, together they form a broader discipleship framework.

The EKI Reading Pathway

Foundations
- *Repent: U-Turns Required* - Kirkland M. Rite *(Coming Soon)*
- *Baptized: Why Did I Get Wet* - Kirkland M. Rite
- *Sozo: What Am I Saved From* - Kirkland M. Rite *(Coming Soon)*

Identity
- *Unchained* - Kirkland M. Rite

Discern the Times & Understand His Voice
- *The Language of Dreams (title forthcoming)* - David S. Webb *(Coming Soon)*
- *I Am the Sign* - Kirkland M. Rite *(Coming Soon)*

Restore the Inner Life
- *Soul Made Whole* - David S. Webb *(Coming Soon)*

Grow Into the New Nature
- *The New Nature Series* - Kirkland M. Rite *(Coming Soon)*

Walk in Kingdom Life
- *Walking in the Kingdom* - David S. Webb *(Coming Soon)*
- *Escape the Shame of Babylon* - David S. Webb
- *The Unique Factor* - David S. Webb

Build Within the Body
- *Building the King Through the Local Church* - David S. Webb
- *Building the Temple to Hold the Glory* - David S. Webb
- *Every Joint Supplieth* - Kirkland M. Rite *(Coming Soon)*

Multiply and Lead
- *Spiritual Fathers (title forthcoming)* - David S. Webb *(Coming Soon)*
- *The Elisha Mandate* - Kirkland M. Rite *(Coming Soon)*

Go Deeper
- *A Gospel of Convicts* - Kirkland M. Rite *(Coming Soon)*
- *The Covenant of Salt* - Kirkland M. Rite *(Coming Soon)*

Foundational and Supplemental Works
- *The Noah Generation* - Kevin Rice
- *Cultivating the New Nature: Growing into the Full Stature of Christ* - Kevin Rice

Companion Resources
- *Values for Living Above and Beyond* - Kevin Rice *(Coming Soon)*

Workbooks and Study Guides - EKI Publishing Team *(Coming Soon)*

Other Works by Kirkland M. Rite:

- *Unchained: Freed to be His Treasure* EKI Publishing 2025

- *Baptized: Why Did I Get Wet* EKI Publishing 2026

- *Sozo: What Am I Saved From?* EKI Publishing 2026

For the Son of man is come to seek and to save
that which was lost.

- Luke 19:10 (KJV)

Dedication:

To those who were taught that salvation was the end of the story yet could not silence the holy ache that there had to be more.

To the hungry, the wounded, the restored, and the still-becoming, may you discover that God's rescue was never meant to end in escape, but to open the way into wholeness, sonship, and the Kingdom of God.

Contents

Prelude

Showing the Way More Perfectly

There is a certain kind of trembling that comes when we talk about salvation. Not a trembling of terror, but a trembling of reverence - the awareness that these are tender words, words people have lived by, prayed with, clung to in hospital rooms, whispered in altar calls, and carried through valleys. Words that hold memories. Words that hold hope.

I approach this book with fear. Not fear of God's judgment, but fear of being misunderstood. So before we step any further, allow me to place this stone of remembrance at the doorway of this book: nothing you are about to read has come to divide you from the faith you already possess. Nothing written here is meant to make you question what God has done in you. The purpose is gentler than that, deeper than that. We are not tearing down; we are unveiling. Not contradicting, but clarifying. Not discarding the path you have walked, but lighting it with a truer flame.

The last thing I want is for any reader to feel as though their faith is being questioned, or their experience dismissed, or their encounter with God reduced to semantics. This book does none of those things.

Let me say this plainly:

I am not here to tell you that you are "not saved."

I am here to help you see what the Scriptures meant when the writers used the word *sozo* [1]- and how rich, layered, and beautiful that word truly is. For many of us, the word "saved" became the entire vocabulary of our beginning with God. It held forgiveness, hope, deliverance, healing, relief. It named the night we wept at an altar, or the afternoon when a verse pierced us, or the morning we felt something shift inside. Those were holy moments. Encounters. Divine interventions. In the ministry of Jesus, such works were not only merciful interventions; they were also witnesses, bearing testimony that the Father had sent Him (John 5:36). We often called those moments "being saved," but Scripture uses the word *sozo* in a broader, more concrete, and more contextual way than our inherited religious language often allows (Mark 5:34; Luke 8:36; Matthew 14:30; James 5:15). Some of those encounters were moments of healing or deliverance, but many were moments of awakening - the Father stirring, inviting, drawing, planting the first seeds of a life that would one day bear the fruit of true restoration.

---

[1] *Sozo* (Greek: σώζω) is the New Testament verb commonly translated "save," but its biblical usage is broader than the modern religious sense often attached to that word. Depending on context, it can mean to rescue, heal, restore, deliver, preserve, or make whole (e.g., Matt. 14:30; Mark 5:34; Luke 8:36; James 5:15). In Scripture, these acts of saving intervention do not automatically carry every other salvific reality into themselves. The New Testament also distinguishes remission of sins, new birth, entrance into the Kingdom, sonship, and inheritance in their own terms and contexts (Matt. 26:28; John 3:3–5; John 1:12–13; Rom. 8:14–17). In this book, sozo refers to a specific act of divine intervention by which God rescues or restores what is threatened, broken, or lost.

Behind and beneath those moments is the Father's deeper intention: that we grow up as sons and daughters in His house. Behind every act of *sozo* is not power alone, but love - agape, the self-giving heart of God moving toward what is broken, bound, drowning, bleeding, scattered, and slipping toward ruin. Heaven does not rescue merely because it can. Heaven rescues because love will not stand at a distance while what belongs to the Father is devoured by death. Every healing, every deliverance, every restoration, every interruption of destruction is love stepping into history. *Sozo* is not cold intervention. It is the Father's heart reaching through the wreckage, not only to pull sons and daughters out of danger, but to bring them home, make them whole, and raise them into maturity. Rescue is love in motion. Sonship is where that love was always headed.

For generations, the Church has handed us a single definition, and with the purest sincerity, many of us built our entire language of faith around it. But what if the Bible's language was even bigger than the one we inherited?

When Priscilla and Aquila heard Apollos preach, he was passionate, accurate, eloquent - and incomplete. Scripture says they *"took him aside, and expounded unto him the way of God more perfectly"* (Acts 18:24–26). They did not rebuke him. They did not dishonor him. They did not undo the good God had already done in him. They simply opened the door to more.

That is the heart of this book. You have not believed wrongly; you have believed partially. And there is no shame in that. Everyone in Scripture - every apostle, every preacher, every disciple - learned in layers. Faith expands. Language matures. Understanding grows.

So, as we explore the difference between rescue and sonship, between the acts by which God rescues us and the larger horizon of God's saving work into which those acts belong, and the inheritance He intends for His sons and daughters, hear this clearly: Nothing here negates your walk with God. Nothing here diminishes what He has done in you. Nothing here suggests you must begin again.

Instead, think of this as a reframing - a deepening, a widening of the horizon, a more accurate vocabulary for what you have already tasted.

Many of us were taught to treat "being saved" as the central defining moment of faith. But in Scripture, the moments we call "saved" are often God's rescuing acts - beautiful, necessary, holy - and yet they are not the whole story. In Christ, they are also signs and witnesses that the Kingdom of God has drawn near (John 5:36). Scripture can speak of rescue, healing, deliverance, and restoration with the language of *sozo*, while still distinguishing those acts from remission of sins, new birth, entrance into the Kingdom, and the inheritance of sons (John 3:3–5; John 1:12–13; Romans 8:14–17). If you have experienced forgiveness, healing, deliverance, or restoration at any point in your life, you have already brushed against the work Scripture calls *sozo* - the restoring touch of God breaking into your story. This book will not take anything from you. It will give language to what God has given you. It will strengthen what you already know. It will explain what you have already experienced. It will reveal why your heart has always sensed that there must be something more.

So step gently with me. Your foundation is not being shaken - it is being expanded. Your faith is not being questioned - it is being clarified. What you have long called salvation is not being undone; it is being more carefully understood within the larger story of God's work. Welcome to the way more perfectly.

Part I

The Problem with the Modern Gospel

Before we can speak clearly about what the gospel is, we must be honest about what it has quietly become.

For many of us, the gospel we inherited was sincere, heartfelt, and deeply meaningful. It brought comfort in grief, hope in fear, and assurance in uncertainty. It gave language to forgiveness and confidence about the future. For that, we should be grateful.

But gratitude does not require silence.

Because alongside that sincerity, something else developed - something subtle, unintended, and rarely questioned. The gospel slowly narrowed. Its center of gravity shifted. And without realizing it, the Church began telling a story that sounded biblical, felt spiritual, and yet moved in a different direction than the one Jesus proclaimed (Mark 1:14–15; Matthew 4:17). In that shift, the saving works of Christ were often retained as cherished stories, yet severed from their fuller function as witnesses that the Father had sent Him and that the Kingdom had truly drawn near (John 5:36).

This section is not written to accuse. It is written to diagnose.

Part I of this book is concerned with a single question: How did the gospel we preach come to focus so heavily on being saved, while saying so little about the Kingdom Jesus announced?

That question is uncomfortable - not because it attacks faith, but because it asks us to examine language we have long assumed was settled. It invites us to distinguish between Scripture itself and the explanations we inherited about Scripture. It also asks us to distinguish between realities Scripture often names separately - rescue, remission, new birth, entry into the Kingdom, sonship, and inheritance - which later tradition has often compressed into one undifferentiated use of salvation language (John 3:3–5; Romans 8:14–17). And it challenges us to consider whether our certainty has sometimes come at the cost of clarity.

In these opening chapters, we will look honestly at how tradition - often well-intentioned and deeply cherished—can shape the way we read the Bible until familiar words no longer mean what they once did (Mark 7:13). We will explore how the language of salvation came to be treated as the goal of the gospel, rather than as part of the way God enacts, reveals, and bears witness to His Kingdom on the earth. And we will examine how this shift has affected the way we think about faith, obedience, baptism, sonship, and inheritance. What Christ's blood accomplished, what birth from above makes possible, what being born of water and Spirit grants, and what the Spirit empowers are not rival truths - but neither are they identical.

This is not a rejection of the gospel you believed. It is an invitation to place that belief back into the larger story Scripture is telling.

If there is tension here, that is intentional. Growth often begins with tension - the moment when inherited answers no longer satisfy the questions Scripture itself is asking. But tension does not mean collapse. It means something is being stretched to hold more.

Part I is not where we build. It is where we clear the ground.

We will name the problem carefully, slowly, and respectfully - because only what is named can be examined, and only what is examined can be healed.

So read these chapters without defensiveness and without fear. Nothing is being taken from you here. What follows is meant to prepare you for what comes next.

Because the gospel Jesus preached was never small, and the saving acts within it were never meant to replace the Kingdom they revealed. The story Scripture is telling is far larger than we were taught to expect.

Scripture Index:

- Mark 1:14–15
- Matthew 4:17
- John 5:36
- Mark 7:13
- John 3:3–5
- Romans 8:14–17

Chapter One

The Gospel We Learned, and the Gospel Jesus Preached

Most of us did not choose the gospel we first believed. We inherited it.

It came to us through trusted voices - pastors we loved, parents who prayed for us, teachers who stood behind pulpits with trembling hands and sincere hearts. It came wrapped in altar calls and sinner's prayers, in whispered assurances and urgent warnings, in simple formulas meant to help us grasp something eternal in the span of a few minutes. And for many of us, it worked - not because it was complete, but because God is gracious.

We were told the gospel was about being saved. Saved from sin. Saved from judgment. Saved from hell. Saved for heaven.

And so modern salvation language became the center of everything. It was the beginning, the middle, and the end. It was the question we asked strangers. It was the moment we pointed to. It was the language we used to describe our standing with God. "I got saved." "Are you saved?" "When were you saved?"

But there is a strange thing that happens when we read the Gospels slowly, without rushing to the familiar words. Jesus rarely speaks the way we learned to speak. He does not preach sermons about "getting saved." He does not invite crowds to secure their afterlife. He does not frame His message around escape. Instead, He opens His mouth and announces something altogether different:

"The time is fulfilled, and the kingdom of God is at hand" (Mark 1:14–15; Matthew 4:17).

That sentence should arrest us.

Jesus did not come announcing a destination. He announced a reign. He did not preach about how to leave the earth. He preached about the will and rule of heaven breaking into it (Matthew 6:10). This is not a small difference. It is a shift so profound that once you see it, you cannot unsee it. The gospel Jesus preached was not primarily about where people would go when they died, but about who they could become while they lived. He spoke of captives released, eyes opened, bodies healed, hearts awakened, and lives reordered under the rule of God (Luke 4:18–19; Matthew 11:4–5; Matthew 12:28).

When people encountered Jesus, they did not ask, "How do I get saved?" They asked, "What shall I do to inherit eternal life?" "What does it mean to follow you?" "How can I see the kingdom of God?" (Luke 10:25; Luke 18:18; Matthew 8:19; John 3:3). Even when Jesus spoke of eternal life, He described it not merely as a future location, but as a present quality of life—life that knows God, walks with Him, and shares in His rule (John 17:3).

Somewhere along the way, the Church began to tell a different story. A well-meaning story. A simpler story. A story designed to answer urgent questions with clear lines and quick conclusions. In that story, modern salvation language became the goal, belief became the requirement, and heaven became the reward. The gospel was reduced to a transaction, and faith was narrowed to agreement.

And yet, when we place that story beside the one told by Jesus and the apostles, cracks begin to appear.

The New Testament uses the word *sozo* - often translated "saved" - in ways that do not fit neatly into our modern categories. A woman is *sozo'd* when her body is healed (Mark 5:34; Luke 8:48). A man cries to be *sozo'd* when he is sinking in the sea (Matthew 14:30). A demoniac is described in the language of being saved when he is restored after oppression (Luke 8:36). The sick are spoken of with this same saving language when healing comes (James 5:15). Even those facing physical destruction can be described in terms of being saved (Acts 27:20, 31, 34). In each case, God intervenes. Something broken is restored. Something threatened is preserved. Something lost is recovered. [2]

And in the ministry of Jesus, those works were not only merciful acts. They were also witnesses. *"The works which the Father hath given me to finish, the same works that I do, bear witness of me"* (John 5:36). The saving acts were part of the testimony.

---

[2] For a detailed categorization of the use of sozo in scripture refer to Appendix A

But notice what *sozo* does not automatically confer.

Being healed does not make someone a son. Being rescued does not grant inheritance. Being delivered does not establish identity. Scripture speaks of sonship, adoption, and inheritance in their own terms, not as automatic byproducts of every act of rescue (John 1:12–13; Romans 8:14–17; Galatians 4:4–7).

These are acts of divine intervention - beautiful, necessary, holy acts - but they are not the destination. They are signs of something greater at work. They are evidence that the kingdom is near (Matthew 12:28; John 5:36), not proof that one has entered its fullness (John 3:3–5).

This is why Jesus could heal ten lepers, and only one would return with deeper recognition (Luke 17:12–19). Why crowds could follow Him for miracles and still walk away from His words (John 6:26, 66). Why people could taste *"the powers of the world to come"* and still stand in danger if they did not continue toward maturity (Hebrews 6:4–5). A saving act can happen in a moment. Sonship is formed over time.

The apostles understood this distinction instinctively. Hebrews does not present Christ's work as merely producing relieved people, but as bringing "many sons unto glory" (Hebrews 2:10). John does not say that belief, in itself, collapses every stage of God's work into one completed reality; he says that receiving Christ grants the authority to become the sons of God (John 1:12–13). And Hebrews does not speak of sons as static, but as those who are disciplined, shaped, and trained by the Father (Hebrews 12:5–11).

This does not diminish the broader biblical reality we call salvation. It restores proper order to our language.

The saving act is not the gospel. It is one of the things the gospel produces.

The gospel is the announcement that God has taken back His world through His Son, that the reign of heaven has broken into human history, and that men and women are being invited not merely to be rescued, but to be born from above, born of water and Spirit, adopted, formed, and entrusted with the inheritance of the kingdom (Mark 1:14–15; John 3:3–5; Romans 8:15–17).

This chapter is concerned chiefly with *sozo* as the saving act—rescue, healing, deliverance, restoration. The broader salvation horizon that Scripture can also speak of in *sōtēria* will be handled more fully later. Here, the point is simpler: the saving act is real, powerful, and necessary, but it is not the whole architecture of the gospel.

When the modern salvation framework is treated as the finish line, growth becomes optional. Transformation becomes secondary. Sonship becomes symbolic. The Christian life collapses into maintenance mode - secure, but shallow. Forgiven, but undeveloped. Comforted, but not commissioned. But when the saving act is understood within a much larger Kingdom story, everything changes. Healing becomes a signpost. Deliverance becomes an invitation. Forgiveness becomes the clearing of ground. Each act of *sozo* whispers the same question beneath it: Will you come further?

This book is not about redefining salvation to make it smaller. It is about placing our salvation language back inside the story that makes it meaningful.

The gospel Jesus preached did not end with rescue. It began there.

And if your heart has ever sensed that the story you were given felt unfinished - if what you were taught to call salvation felt real but incomplete, powerful but unresolved - you are not alone. You are not deficient. You are not ungrateful.

You may simply be standing at the place where rescue gives way to calling, mercy opens into sonship, and the witness of Christ's works beckons you beyond relief into kingdom life.

And that is where the real story begins.

Scripture Index:

- Mark 1:14–15
- Matthew 4:17
- Matthew 6:10
- Luke 4:18–19
- Matthew 11:4–5
- Matthew 12:28
- Luke 10:25
- Luke 18:18
- Matthew 8:19
- John 3:3
- John 17:3
- Mark 5:34

- Luke 8:48
- Matthew 14:30
- Luke 8:36
- James 5:15
- Acts 27:20
- Acts 27:31
- Acts 27:34
- John 5:36
- John 1:12–13
- Romans 8:14–17
- Galatians 4:4–7
- John 3:3–5
- Luke 17:12–19
- John 6:26
- John 6:66
- Hebrews 6:4–5
- Hebrews 2:10
- Hebrews 12:5–11
- Romans 8:15–17

Chapter Two

How Tradition Made the Word of God of No Effect

Jesus once said something so unsettling that it still makes us uncomfortable to read out loud:

"You have made the word of God of none effect through your tradition" (Mark 7:13).

He did not say this to pagans. He did not say it to unbelievers. He said it to the most Scripture-saturated people of His day.

That alone should slow us down.

Because if tradition could empty the Word of its effect, then, it can do so now - not through rebellion, but through devotion to inherited forms. Not through rejection of Scripture, but through loyalty to inherited interpretation.

Tradition does not usually announce itself as tradition. It presents itself as faithfulness.

Tradition Is Not the Enemy - Confusion Is

Jesus was not anti-tradition.

He observed feasts. He attended synagogue. He quoted Scripture fluently.

What He confronted was something more subtle: when inherited explanation begins to override revelation, and interpretation becomes a substitute for obedience.

Tradition becomes dangerous not when it exists, but when it begins to redefine words God has already spoken, to close what Scripture leaves open (Matthew 23:13), or to conclude what God intended to unfold.

When that happens, Scripture is still read, still honored, still defended - but it quietly loses its power to confront, to heal, to restore, and to transform.

The Word remains true. It simply becomes ineffective.

How Words Lose Their Weight

Words are not static. They travel.

They move across languages, cultures, centuries, and systems. And when they do, their meaning can shift - not through malice, but through repeated use.

This is how a word like *sozo* - once heard in contexts of healing, rescue, restoration, and deliverance - can slowly be reduced to a single idea: going to heaven when you die.

Nothing in the word itself demanded that reduction. Nothing in the Gospel required it.

But tradition, once established, is powerful. It trains us not only how to read Scripture, but what we are permitted to hear when we read it.

That is why precision matters. If *sozo* is collapsed into a single final meaning, then the saving act is confused with the broader salvation horizon. A concrete act of rescue is made to carry realities Scripture often names more carefully in other terms - remission, new birth, Kingdom entry, sonship, and inheritance. The result is not greater clarity, but theological compression.

When Tradition Becomes the Lens

By the time Jesus arrived, Israel had Scripture, commentary, commentary on commentary, and rules built to protect rules built to protect rules.

The irony is painful.

The Word made flesh stood before them - healing, restoring, forgiving, delivering - and they debated definitions.

They knew the text. They missed the moment.

Tradition did not remove Scripture from their hands. It filtered Scripture through expectation until nothing new could pass through.

That is the danger we must acknowledge if we are to read honestly.

Paul later described this same problem using different language. He spoke of a veil.

In 2 Corinthians 3:14–16, Paul says that when Moses is read, a veil remains upon the heart. His point is not that Moses is defective, nor that the text lacks clarity in itself. His point is that something can stand between the reader and what the text is actually revealing in Christ. The words are heard. The sentences are understood. The Scriptures are honored. And yet the true unveiling is still resisted.

This is why Paul's language is so important. The veil is not first over the page, but over the heart. It is not removed by familiarity with the text, by more confident repetition, or by inherited certainty. It is removed "when it shall turn to the Lord" (2 Corinthians 3:16). In other words, revelation requires more than possession of the text; it requires turning toward the One to whom the text bears witness.

This is what unchecked tradition can do. It does not silence Scripture outright. It allows Scripture to be read while preventing it from being seen. It lets the words pass through familiar pathways until nothing disruptive, searching, or enlarging can break through. Even the promises of Christ can remain on the page while expectation is quietly reduced beneath them (John 14:12).

The danger is not that we stop reading the Bible. The danger is that we read it through a veil.

The Subtle Cost of Familiar Language

Tradition rarely announces itself with error. It announces itself with certainty.

Phrases get repeated. Definitions get assumed. Questions stop being asked.

Before long, the language of salvation is made to carry everything at once. The saving act is mistaken for the whole story. Rescue is treated as though it were the goal itself, rather than one of the ways God enacts and reveals His Kingdom on the earth. Faith becomes agreement instead of allegiance. Grace becomes a force instead of favor. The Kingdom becomes distant instead of present.

Scripture is still quoted. But its edges are dulled.

This is what Jesus meant by *"making the word of God of no effect"* (Mark 7:13).

Why This Matters Now

This book is not an attack on the Church. It is not a rejection of the faith handed down to us. It is an invitation to do what Jesus Himself did:

to return to the words, to listen without filters, and to let Scripture speak again before tradition explains it away.

If tradition has redefined *sozo*, then our language about salvation must be reexamined. If tradition has reduced baptism, then obedience must be restored. If tradition has narrowed the gospel, then the Kingdom must be brought back into view. And if tradition has blurred the distinction between the saving act and the broader salvation horizon, then our language must be disciplined until Scripture is allowed to name things in their own order again.

Not to discard what we have believed - but to see it more perfectly.

A Necessary Posture

This chapter requires humility.

Because tradition is easiest to see in someone else's theology. Harder to see in our own language. Hardest to see in the words we have never questioned.

But Jesus' warning was not cruel. It was merciful.

He was not trying to shame His hearers. He was trying to free them.

And freedom begins when we allow the Word to speak before we decide what it must mean.

Scripture Index:

- Mark 7:13
- Matthew 23:13
- 2 Corinthians 3:14–16
- 2 Corinthians 3:16
- John 14:12

Chapter Three

The Ferrari in the Garage:

Why Rescue Is Not the Same as Inheritance

There is a quiet assumption many of us inherited without realizing it.

We were taught - sometimes explicitly, sometimes by implication - that once a person is "saved," everything God possesses is now open to them by default: heaven, authority, inheritance, the Father's house.

But Scripture does not speak that simply.

The New Testament often uses *sozo* to name a saving act: rescue, healing, deliverance, restoration, preservation. Those acts are real. They are merciful. They are necessary. But the saving act, by itself, is not the same thing as inheritance.

To confuse rescue with inheritance is to misunderstand both.

The Garage That Isn't Yours

Imagine this.

A man owns a home with a garage. Inside that garage sits a Ferrari - immaculate, powerful, expensive, unmistakably his. If someone breaks into that garage, takes the car, and drives it down the street, they are guilty of theft. No amount of appreciation for the car changes that reality.

Now imagine something different.

The owner adopts that person as a son.

The garage door opens again. The same car sits inside. But now, when the son takes the keys and drives away, nothing unlawful has occurred. The difference was not the car. The difference was relationship.

What changed was not the value of the thing accessed, but the standing of the one who received it.

This is where much confusion enters our theology.

Rescue Is Not Adoption

The New Testament uses the language of *sozo* - rescue, healing, deliverance, restoration - freely and often. People are *sozo'd* from sickness, danger, oppression, and destruction (Mark 5:34; Matthew 14:30; Luke 8:36; James 5:15).

But *sozo* language does not automatically include adoption language.

A person rescued from drowning does not become the heir of the lifeguard.

A prisoner released from captivity does not become the child of the one who opened the cell.

Rescue restores life. Adoption establishes family standing. Scripture does not flatten these into the same category.

Inheritance Is Spoken of in the Language of Family

Paul is careful with his words.

He does not frame inheritance in the abstract language of the "saved," but in the familial language of sons and children: "if children, then heirs" (Romans 8:14–17; Galatians 4:4–7). "If children, then heirs; heirs of God, and joint-heirs with Christ" (Romans 8:17).

Inheritance flows from family identity, not merely from divine intervention.

This is why Scripture repeatedly speaks of adoption, sonship, maturity, formation, and conformity to the image of Christ (Romans 8:29; Galatians 4:4–7; Hebrews 2:10). These are not decorative ideas. They are directional.

God is not merely performing saving acts. He is bringing many sons to glory (Hebrews 2:10).

Why Jesus Did Not Preach a Gospel of Immediate Entitlement

Jesus did not go from town to town offering automatic inheritance to everyone who experienced His power.

He spoke instead of sons in the Father's house (John 8:35), servants becoming friends through revealed relationship (John 15:15), stewards entrusted with responsibility (Luke 12:42–44), and a little flock to whom the Father is pleased to give the kingdom (Luke 12:32).

Even His parables make the distinction clear.

Many are invited. Few are entrusted.

Power without formation destroys. Privilege without sonship corrupts.

This is why Jesus did not simply perform saving acts and move on. He called people to follow, to learn, to obey, and to be shaped (Matthew 4:19; Matthew 11:29; Luke 9:23).

The saving act interrupts destruction. Sonship prepares for inheritance.

The Cost of Confusing the Two

When rescue is treated as though it were already the full inheritance, several things quietly disappear.

Inheritance becomes assumed instead of awaited and prepared for. Maturity becomes optional. Discipleship becomes secondary. Authority is claimed without formation.

We end up with people who are grateful to be rescued, but unprepared to rule.

Scripture does not speak of inheritance as the automatic result of every saving act. It speaks of inheritance in the language of children, sons, and heirs (Romans 8:14–17; Galatians 4:4–7).

Why This Matters More Than We Think

If every act of *sozo* carried the same standing as sonship, then healing from cancer would place a person in the same category as adoption into God's family. Scripture does not say this.

Acts of *sozo* are real. They are powerful. They are merciful. But they do not, by themselves, redefine identity.

Scripture speaks of sonship in its own terms. *"As many as received him, to them gave he power to become the sons of God"* (John 1:12–13). "As many as are led by the Spirit of God, they are the sons of God" (Romans 8:14). *"Because ye are sons, God hath sent forth the Spirit of his Son into your hearts"* (Galatians 4:6).

And sonship is not treated as casual language. It is bound up with relationship, leading, discipline, maturity, and glory. This is why the New Testament speaks of believers being led by the Spirit (Romans 8:14), disciplined by the Father (Hebrews 12:5–11), trained in righteousness (2 Timothy 3:16–17), and prepared for glory (Hebrews 2:10).

God is not stockpiling rescued people. He is raising sons.

Rescue Is Not the End of the Story

The saving act matters deeply. Without rescue, there is no life to grow. Without divine intervention, there is no future to inherit.

But rescue is not the garage key.

It is the hand that pulls you from the wreck, sets you upright, and invites you into a house where something far greater is being prepared.

This chapter is concerned with *sozo* as saving act, not with the whole sweep of *sōtēria* as the broader salvation horizon. The point here is not that rescue is small, but that rescue is not the whole architecture of inheritance.

The gospel does not end with rescue.

It moves toward becoming a son.

And sons inherit.

Scripture Index :

- Mark 5:34
- Matthew 14:30
- Luke 8:36
- James 5:15
- Romans 8:14–17
- Galatians 4:4–7
- Romans 8:17
- Romans 8:29
- Hebrews 2:10
- John 8:35
- John 15:15
- Luke 12:42–44
- Luke 12:32
- Matthew 4:19
- Matthew 11:29
- Luke 9:23
- John 1:12–13
- Romans 8:14
- Galatians 4:6
- Hebrews 12:5–11
- 2 Timothy 3:16–17

Part II

What Sozo Actually is in the Bible

By this point, one thing should be clear: the word salvation, especially as we have inherited it in modern church language, has been asked to carry far more weight than Scripture itself always places on it.

In Part I, we examined how tradition can quietly reshape familiar language until the words of Scripture no longer function as they once did. We saw how the gospel slowly narrowed, how salvation language was repositioned, and how the saving act was often mistaken for inheritance.

Now we must do something more difficult—and more hopeful.

We must let the Bible define its own words again.

Part II of this book is not interested in theological systems, denominational formulations, or inherited summaries of belief. It is concerned with usage. With context. With how Scripture itself employs the language of being saved in real situations, spoken to real people, facing real conditions.

When the New Testament uses the word *sozo*, it is not vague. It is not abstract. It names concrete acts of rescue, healing, deliverance, restoration, and preservation. And those acts are rarely singular.

People are saved from things. Saved in moments. Saved in ways that are visible, specific, and textually grounded.

A man is saved from demonic oppression (Luke 8:36). A woman is saved from disease (Mark 5:34). A child is spoken of in the language of being saved from death (Mark 5:23). A community is preserved from destruction (Acts 27:20, 31, 34). A people are spoken of as saved from judgment (Romans 5:9).

These saving acts are not metaphors for the afterlife. They are interventions of God's power and mercy into present reality.

And in the ministry of Jesus, they are more than merciful acts alone. They are also witnesses. *The works which the Father hath given me to finish, the same works that I do, bear witness of me* (John 5:36). The acts of *sozo* do not replace the message of the Kingdom; they testify that the Father sent the Son and that the Kingdom has drawn near.

This section will show, carefully and textually, that *sozo* in Scripture is not a process to be completed, nor a status to be possessed, but a saving act enacted whenever God confronts what destroys His creation.

That does not diminish the larger biblical reality we often call salvation. It clarifies its order.

For Scripture does not always speak with one term alone. *Sozo* often names the saving act itself, while the broader horizon of God's saving work can also be spoken of in other ways, including what the New Testament calls *sōtēria*. This section will begin with the act itself, because before the larger horizon can be understood, the concrete work must first be seen clearly.

As we move through these chapters, you may notice that the Bible speaks of God's saving work far more often than you were taught - but almost never in the way you were taught to hear it. That is not because Scripture is inconsistent. It is because tradition trained us to listen for only one meaning, while the text has often been speaking in many.

Part II is where we slow down. Where we look at the passages themselves. Where we allow the saving acts of God to be as large, as practical, and as powerful as Scripture presents them.

Because before we can talk about remission, new birth, entry into the Kingdom, Spirit-empowered witness, sonship, inheritance, and the Kingdom to come, we must first understand what *sozo* actually does - and what it was never meant to replace.

Scripture Index:

- Luke 8:36
- Mark 5:34
- Mark 5:23
- Acts 27:20
- Acts 27:31
- Acts 27:34
- Romans 5:9
- John 5:36

Chapter Four

Sozo: The Bible's Most Misunderstood Word

There are words we think we know because we have heard them our whole lives.

"Saved" is one of them.

It appears in sermons, testimonies, altar calls, and hymns. It is spoken with gratitude and certainty. It has been prayed over hospital beds and whispered in moments of fear. And because it is familiar, we rarely stop to ask a dangerous question:

Saved from what?

Scripture never treats that question as optional.

A Word That Refuses to Be Singular

The Greek word often translated "save" in the New Testament is *sozo*.

It is not a technical theological term. It is not reserved for altar calls or doctrinal statements. It is an ordinary word, used in ordinary situations, spoken to people facing very real danger, sickness, oppression, and loss.

A woman touches the hem of Jesus' garment and is *sozo'd* (Mark 5:34). A man oppressed by demons is described in the language of being saved when he is restored (Luke 8:36). A child near death is spoken of in the language of being saved (Mark 5:23).

49

A storm threatens to swallow a boat, and the disciples cry out to be saved (Matthew 8:25; Matthew 14:30).

In none of these moments is anyone asking about the afterlife.

They are asking to be rescued. To be healed. To be delivered. To be preserved.

The word refuses to narrow itself.

How We Learned to Hear Only One Meaning

Somewhere along the way, *sozo* was taught to us as a destination.

A single moment. A decisive event. A spiritual status.

Once achieved, it was assumed to contain everything else.

But Scripture does not use the word that way.

The Bible never treats *sozo* as a container holding all of God's work. It treats it as a saving act - something God does when He confronts what threatens His creation.

When we collapse *sozo* into one fixed meaning, we do not make the language of salvation bigger.

We make it smaller.

Sozo in the Mouths of the Apostles

The apostles spoke about God's saving work the way they experienced it.

Paul does not say, "God acted once, and that settled every way Scripture can speak of being saved."

He says: "*Who delivered us from so great a death, and doth deliver: in whom we trust that he will yet deliver us*" (2 Corinthians 1:10).

Past. Present. Future.

Not a process of earning. Not a ladder of progress. But repeated acts of divine intervention.

That is why this chapter is concerned primarily with *sozo* as the saving act. The broader salvation horizon - what Scripture can also describe in *sōtēria* - must not be collapsed into every instance where the text speaks of being saved. The act is real. The horizon is larger. But the two must not be confused.

Why This Matters More Than We Think

If every use of being saved is forced into one singular idea, then the Christian life becomes confusing.

What do we do with healing? With deliverance? With rescue from danger? With preservation in crisis? With restoration after failure?

We either minimize them or force them into a category they were never meant to occupy.

But if *sozo* is allowed to mean what Scripture actually shows it to mean - God's saving act wherever rescue is needed - then the gospel becomes larger, not smaller.

God performs saving acts more than once. More than one way. Against more than one threat.

And He always has.

The Discipline of Letting the Text Speak

This chapter is not asking you to abandon what you have believed.

It is asking you to read more carefully.

To notice when Scripture uses the word *sozo*. To observe the condition being addressed. To resist importing conclusions that are not present in the text.

When the Bible says someone was saved, it very often tells us from what.

That is not accidental. It is instructive.

And in the ministry of Jesus, these acts are not merely merciful interruptions of suffering. They are also witnesses. "*The works which the Father hath given me to finish, the same works that I do, bear witness of me*" (John 5:36). The acts themselves testify. They do not replace the Kingdom message; they reveal that the Father sent the Son and that the Kingdom has drawn near.

A Word That Serves the Kingdom

Sozo was never meant to replace the Kingdom message.

It serves it.

Where God's reign confronts sickness, there is healing. Where it confronts demons, there is deliverance. Where it confronts death, there is life. Where it confronts judgment, there is mercy or deliverance, depending on the context.

The saving act is the Kingdom acting.

Not once. But whenever it is needed.

This is why the works of Jesus matter so much in this discussion. They are not side notes to the message. They are not interruptions of proclamation. They are part of the witness that the reign of God has arrived in Him (Matthew 12:28; John 5:36).

What We Are About to Do

In the chapters that follow, we will let Scripture do what tradition has often prevented it from doing.

We will look at how *sozo* is actually used. We will categorize its occurrences based on context. And we will allow the language of being saved to mean what the text says it means - no more, and no less.

This will not make the broader biblical reality of salvation weaker.

It will make our language truer.

Because a gospel that can only speak of one saving moment is a fragile thing.

But a gospel in which God's reign confronts what destroys life again and again - that is the gospel Scripture has been proclaiming all along.

Scripture Index:

- Mark 5:34
- Luke 8:36
- Mark 5:23
- Matthew 8:25
- Matthew 14:30
- 2 Corinthians 1:10
- John 5:36
- Matthew 12:28

Chapter Five

Sozo Is Not a Process - But God Saves More Than Once

One of the most common misunderstandings in modern salvation language is not only that it is too small, but that it has been given the wrong shape.

We have been taught to imagine salvation as a process - a long spiritual journey that begins with being "saved" and slowly moves toward completion through effort, growth, and time. Language like working out salvation, growing into salvation, or maintaining salvation often reinforces this idea.

But Scripture does not describe *sozo* that way.

The saving act is not something that unfolds gradually. It is something God does.

The Saving Act Is an Intervention, Not a Path

In the Bible, *sozo* is decisive.

A storm threatens a boat, and the disciples cry out to be saved (Matthew 8:25; Matthew 14:30). A disease ravages a body, and healing comes (Mark 5:34; James 5:15). A demon torments a man, and deliverance occurs (Luke 8:36). A people face destruction, and God intervenes (Acts 27:20, 31, 34).

In every case, *sozo* is not progressive. It is interruptive.

God steps in. The condition changes. The threat is confronted.

Sozo does not describe the journey that follows. It describes the moment when divine intervention meets threatened life.

Why *Sozo* Cannot Be a Process

If *sozo* were a process, it would imply that rescue unfolds through effort, deliverance depends on progress, or intervention is conditioned upon development.

Scripture never speaks this way.

Processes require cultivation. *Sozo* names intervention.

The saving act is not achieved. It is received.

Not because merit is assessed, nor because punishment is merely postponed, but because God acts graciously when life is endangered.

And Yet God Saves More Than Once

Here is where clarity matters.

Saying *sozo* is not a process does not mean God acts to save only once.

Paul gives us one of the clearest statements in all of Scripture: "*Who delivered us from so great a death, and doth deliver: in whom we trust that he will yet deliver us*" (2 Corinthians 1:10).

Past. Present. Future.

Not stages of one extended saving act, but repeated interventions by the same saving God.

Each deliverance addresses a real condition. Each act stands complete in its moment. None cancel the others.

God acts again because new threats arise.

Sozo and _Sōtēria_ Are Not the Same Emphasis

At this point, a distinction must be made plainly.

The New Testament does not speak with one word alone. It uses _sozo_ and _sōtēria_, and while the two are related, they do not always carry the same emphasis.

Sozo often names the saving act itself: rescue, healing, deliverance, restoration, preservation. It is concrete. It happens when God intervenes.

Sōtēria, however, can speak with a broader horizon. It can describe salvation as present arrival, ongoing reception, and future unveiling.

Luke can say, _"This day is salvation come to this house"_ (Luke 19:9). Peter can speak of _"receiving the end of your faith, even the salvation of your souls"_ (First Peter 1:9). Paul can say, _"Now is our salvation nearer than when we believed"_ (Romans 13:11). And Hebrews can speak of Christ appearing _"unto salvation"_ for those who wait for Him (Hebrews 9:28).

That is not contradiction. It is biblical precision.

The saving act can be complete in its moment, while the larger saving horizon into which that act belongs is still being received, approached, or awaited.

This is why *sozo* must not be turned into a process, and *sōtēria* must not be flattened into a single moment. One often names the act. The other can name the broader reality, condition, or horizon into which those acts belong.

The Christian Life Is Not the Saving Act

This distinction is essential.

The Christian life is not *sozo*. *Sozo* makes the Christian life possible.

Growth, obedience, formation, discipline, maturity—these are not themselves saving acts. They are the life that unfolds after God has intervened.

When the saving act is confused with the Christian life, it is burdened with expectations it was never meant to carry. And when that happens, we either turn growth into earning or turn stagnation into false security.

Neither reflects Scripture.

Why This Distinction Brings Freedom

When the saving act is understood as intervention rather than process, something liberating happens.

We stop striving to make rescue into a ladder. We stop measuring growth by fear. We stop treating obedience as payment.

And we begin to see God as Scripture presents Him: a God who steps in, a God who rescues again, a God who acts graciously without requiring prior worthiness.

The saving act meets us where destruction threatens. Formation carries us where maturity is required.

Many Saving Acts, One Direction

Although God acts to save many times, His works are never random.

Each saving act moves in the same direction:

away from destruction, toward life, under God's reign.

The saving act clears the threat. The Kingdom establishes order. The Spirit empowers witness. Sonship prepares for inheritance.

These are not competing realities. They are rightly ordered ones.

And in Christ, these saving acts are not merely merciful interventions. They are also witnesses. *"The works which the Father hath given me to finish, the same works that I do, bear witness of me"* (John 5:36). The saving acts do not replace the message of the Kingdom; they testify that the Father sent the Son and that the Kingdom has drawn near.

Why This Matters for What Comes Next

If *sozo* is always a saving act, then the most important question is no longer simply, "Have I been saved?"

It becomes, "What is God saving me from now?"

That question does not diminish faith. It sharpens it.

Because Scripture is not vague about the forces that threaten life. It names them. Describes them. Confronts them.

And that is where we turn next.

Scripture Index:

- Matthew 8:25
- Matthew 14:30
- Mark 5:34
- James 5:15
- Luke 8:36
- Acts 27:20
- Acts 27:31
- Acts 27:34
- 2 Corinthians 1:10
- Luke 19:9
- 1 Peter 1:9
- Romans 13:11
- Hebrews 9:28
- John 5:36

Chapter Six

Saved from What? A Biblical List, Not a Traditional One

If *sozo* names a saving act of divine intervention, then the most honest question Scripture invites us to ask is not first how people are saved, but from what?

The Bible rarely leaves that question vague.

When *sozo* occurs, it has an object. A threat. A condition. Something real that presses against life and must be confronted. Scripture does not speak of the saving act in the abstract. It speaks of it in context.

And when we allow the text to speak without importing later assumptions, a pattern begins to emerge.

This chapter is not yet attempting to map the whole horizon of *sōtēria*. It is tracing the kinds of threats to which *sozo* responds.

Saved from Powers That Enslave

Some people in the Gospels were saved from forces that were not merely internal.

They were tormented. Bound. Dominated by powers they could not overcome by willpower or insight. When Jesus delivered them, Scripture does not describe an inward realization or a merely legal declaration. It describes freedom (Luke 8:36).

Chains fall. Minds clear. Bodies return to their right place. This is *sozo*.

The saving act here is not forgiveness in the abstract. It is the breaking of domination, the restoration of agency, the return of a person to themselves.

Saved from Disease and Bodily Decay

Others came to Jesus carrying sickness in their bodies.

They did not ask philosophical questions. They asked to be made whole. And when healing came, Scripture repeatedly uses the language of being saved. A woman is told her faith has saved her (Mark 5:34). A blind man receives sight and is told the same (Luke 18:42). The sick are spoken of in this same saving language when healing comes (James 5:15).

These moments are not metaphors for something else. They are saving acts enacted in flesh.

The Kingdom does not bypass the body. It confronts what destroys it.

Saved from Death and Destruction

Sometimes the saving act arrives just in time.

A storm rises. A child lies dying. A people face annihilation.

In these moments, Scripture speaks plainly. The disciples cry out to be saved from the storm (Matthew 8:25). Jairus pleads that his little daughter may be saved and live (Mark 5:23). Those on the ship in Acts are described in the language of being saved from destruction (Acts 27:20, 31, 34).

Here, *sozo* is rescue from immediate loss of life.

Not symbolically. Not eventually. But concretely.

Saved from Sin's Grip

There are moments when the saving act addresses not only an external threat, but an internal bondage.

Sin in Scripture is not treated merely as guilt. It is also described as a power that enslaves, corrupts, and deforms. When God acts to save here, it is not simply pardon. It is release.

"He shall save his people from their sins" (Matthew 1:21). A sinful woman hears, *"Thy faith hath saved thee; go in peace"* (Luke 7:50). And Jesus declares that the Son of Man came *"to seek and to save that which was lost"* (Luke 19:10). James adds that the one who turns a sinner from the error of his way *"shall save a soul from death"* (James 5:20).

The sinner is forgiven, yes - but more than that, restored. Reoriented. Returned toward right relationship with God and others.

The saving act here is not merely a legal transaction. It is a relational repair and a moral reordering.

Saved from Shame and Exile

Some forms of destruction are quieter.

Shame isolates. Exile removes belonging. Honor is lost, and with it, place in the community.

Scripture also shows saving acts restoring honor, covering shame, and bringing the outcast home. A woman long marked by uncleanness is publicly restored, not only in body but in dignity (Mark 5:34). A leper is not merely healed, but returned from exclusion with the language of being made whole (Luke 17:19).

When God acts here, He does not merely change a person's feelings. He repositions them.

The shamed are clothed. The excluded are welcomed. The forgotten are named.

This too is *sozo*.

Saved from Judgment and Wrath

There are passages where the language of being saved clearly addresses judgment.

But even here, the language must be handled carefully.

Scripture speaks of God saving people from coming wrath - not as an abstract hellscape, but as real consequences unfolding in history and beyond it (Romans 5:9–10; 1 Thessalonians 5:9). Judgment in Scripture is not merely punitive. It also exposes, corrects, and reorders.

The saving act here does not erase responsibility. It redirects the outcome.

God intervenes so that destruction does not have the final word.

A Pattern Emerges

When we place these passages side by side, something becomes clear.

Sozo in Scripture is not aimed at a single problem. It confronts many threats.

Demonic oppression. Disease. Death. Destruction. Bondage. Shame. Judgment.

Each saving act addresses a specific condition. None are symbolic stand-ins for something else. None collapse into a single category.

This is why the language of being saved must be allowed to be plural in its applications.

And in the ministry of Jesus, these acts are more than merciful interventions. They are also witnesses. *"The works which the Father hath given me to finish, the same works that I do, bear witness of me"* (John 5:36). They testify that the Father sent the Son and that the Kingdom has drawn near (Matthew 12:28).

Why the List Matters

When the language of being saved is reduced to one thing, the gospel becomes fragile.

If being saved only means escape from hell, then healing becomes an embarrassing add-on or disappears from expectation altogether. Deliverance becomes suspect. Restoration becomes secondary. And vast portions of Scripture are quietly sidelined.

But when *sozo* is allowed to mean what Scripture shows it to mean, the gospel becomes robust.

God acts to save wherever life is threatened. And He does so again and again.

What This Prepares Us For

This chapter does not conclude the conversation. It sharpens it.

Because once we see what *sozo* addresses, we must ask a deeper question:

If God acts to save from all these things, what is He saving us for?

The saving act clears threats. But it is not the destination.

And that is where the story moves next.

Scripture Index:

- Luke 8:36
- Mark 5:34
- Luke 18:42
- James 5:15

- Matthew 8:25
- Mark 5:23
- Acts 27:20
- Acts 27:31
- Acts 27:34
- Matthew 1:21
- Luke 7:50
- Luke 19:9–10
- Luke 17:19
- Romans 5:9–10
- 1 Thessalonians 5:9
- John 5:36
- Matthew 12:28

Part III

The Missing Pieces: New Birth, Sonship, and Inheritance

By this point, one thing should be unmistakable: the saving act is not the destination of the gospel.

It is essential. It is powerful. And it is never the end of the story.

In the previous section, we allowed the Bible to speak plainly about what *sozo* actually does - divine intervention wherever life is threatened. We saw that Scripture uses the language of being saved repeatedly, situationally, and concretely. God acts to save people from many things, many times, because the threats against life are many.

But rescue alone does not explain why Jesus came.

The saving act clears danger. It does not, by itself, define identity.

This is where much of the modern conversation quietly stops - and where the New Testament keeps going.

Jesus did not say we must be saved to see the Kingdom. He said, "Except a man be born again, he cannot see the kingdom of God," and, "Except a man be born of water and of the Spirit, he cannot enter into the kingdom of God" (John 3:3–5).

That distinction matters.

Birth does not rescue someone from danger. Birth brings someone into life.

It grants capacity. It establishes identity. It opens a future.

In Part III, we turn our attention to what Scripture presents as the next movement in God's purpose - not as an optional upgrade to rescue, but as part of the very reason God acts to save in the first place.

The New Testament does not aim at producing rescued people who remain perpetual dependents.

It speaks instead of sons and daughters, heirs and joint-heirs, the Firstborn among many brethren, and a family prepared to share in God's reign (Romans 8:14–17, 29; Galatians 4:4–7; Hebrews 2:10–11).

This language is not poetic filler. It is structural.

Paul does not frame adoption as a decorative metaphor. He presents sonship and heirship as central to God's purpose in Christ (Romans 8:14–17; Galatians 4:4–7). Inheritance is not an abstract reward. It is tied to resurrection, maturity, and authority. And sonship is not merely announced in the language of family - it is also formed through the life of that family (Hebrews 12:5–11).

Part III is where we name what has often been left unnamed.

We will explore why new birth is not identical to the saving act, but the beginning of Kingdom capacity. We will explore why sonship - not rescue alone - is the stated aim of Christ's work. We will explore why formation, discipline, and obedience are not threats to grace, but evidence of family life. And we will explore why inheritance - shared rule with Christ - is the horizon toward which Scripture consistently points.

Nothing here diminishes the broader biblical reality we call salvation. It explains why God's saving work matters.

The saving act makes life possible. Birth opens Kingdom capacity. Sonship prepares for inheritance.

This is not about striving to become something you are not. It is about recognizing what God has been moving toward all along.

Part III does not introduce a new gospel. It restores the trajectory of the one Jesus preached.

And it begins where Jesus began - not with rescue alone, but with birth.

Scripture Index:

- John 3:3–5
- Romans 8:14–17
- Romans 8:29
- Galatians 4:4–7
- Hebrews 2:10–11
- Hebrews 12:5–11

Chapter Seven

New Birth Is Not The Saving Act

Few phrases in Scripture have been so universally quoted - and so quietly misunderstood - as the words born again.

They have become shorthand for conversion, synonymous with what many modern believers mean by "being saved," treated as the moment when everything changes and the story is complete. For many believers, new birth is where the gospel ends.

But Jesus did not speak of it that way.

When He introduced the concept, He was not answering a question about rescue. He was explaining capacity - and the beginning of life that can grow within the Kingdom toward maturity.

Jesus' Words, Not Ours

Jesus did not say, "Unless one is born again, he cannot be saved."

He said, *"Except a man be born again, he cannot see the kingdom of God"* (John 3:3).

And again, *"Except a man be born of water and of the Spirit, he cannot enter into the kingdom of God"* (John 3:5).

These are not interchangeable ideas.

Seeing is not rescue. Entering is not deliverance. Birth is not the saving act.

Jesus was not describing a moment when danger is removed. He was describing the means by which perception and participation become possible.

Birth, in every sense, creates capacity. It does not solve every problem. It begins life.

Why the Confusion Took Hold

The modern church often speaks of new birth as though it answers every question at once.

Forgiveness? New birth. Rescue? New birth. Eternal life? New birth.

But Scripture uses different language for different realities, and when those distinctions collapse, clarity is lost.

New birth became convenient. Salvation language became compressed. Identity was mistaken for rescue.

The result is a gospel that speaks fluently about beginnings, but rarely about growth, formation, or inheritance.

When this book speaks of formation, it does not refer to what is commonly called "spiritual formation" [3] in modern

---

[3] Here "spiritual formation" refers to the modern evangelical-academic and contemplative usage associated especially with Richard J. Foster, Dallas Willard, and the Renovaré movement, not to the biblical pattern of familial training toward sonship, maturity, and inheritance used in this book. Foster and Renovaré explicitly frame this discourse in terms of the contemplative tradition and meditative prayer, while Willard defines spiritual formation with strong

academic or contemplative theology. It does not describe self-cultivation through inward techniques or disciplines as ends in themselves. Formation, as Scripture presents it, is the family work of God - the training and preparation of sons for maturity, responsibility, and inheritance. It is not about becoming worthy. It is about becoming capable.

Birth Is Not Rescue

No one confuses being born with being rescued in ordinary life.

A child born into the world has not thereby been delivered from every danger. They have been brought into life. Birth does not guarantee safety, maturity, or success. It makes growth possible.

Jesus' language follows the same logic.

New birth does not, by itself, free someone from sickness, oppression, or death. It gives them the capacity to see, respond to, and participate in God's reign.

The saving act intervenes when destruction threatens. Birth introduces a person into a realm where life can grow.

---

philosophical and psychological categories, including the formation of the human spirit or will and the use of psychological research in relation to spiritual disciplines. This note does not claim direct dependence upon Taoism as a documented source, but it does mark the modern spiritual formation movement as a distinct framework shaped by contemplative retrieval and philosophical-psychological anthropology rather than by the biblical categories governing this work.

These are related - but they are not the same.

Water and Spirit: A Beginning, Not a Conclusion

When Jesus speaks of being born of water and Spirit, He is not outlining a symbolic ritual or a theological shortcut.

He is describing origin and entry.

Birth from above grants sight of the Kingdom (John 3:3). Birth of water and Spirit grants entry into it (John 3:5).

Water here marks cleansing, transition, and entry. Spirit marks life, animation, and divine source.

Together, they mark the beginning of Kingdom life - not its completion.

To be born of water and Spirit is not to stand at the finish line. It is to stand at the threshold of a life that must still grow.

Saving Acts Attend the New Birth, but Do Not Exhaust It

None of this means that new birth is empty, symbolic, or without tangible effect.

On the contrary, Scripture speaks of real acts of God attending the beginning of Kingdom life. Peter can say, *"The like figure whereunto even baptism doth also now save us"* (First Peter 3:21). Paul can speak of *"the washing of regeneration, and renewing of the Holy Ghost"* (Titus 3:5). Ezekiel had already prophesied in this direction: *"Then will I sprinkle clean water upon you, and ye shall be clean... A new heart also will I give you, and a new spirit will I put within you"* (Ezekiel 36:25–27).

These are not empty signs. They are real acts of God. Cleansing is real. Renewal is real. The conscience is addressed. The heart is touched. The old order is broken, and a new order begins.

But that is precisely the point: these saving acts do not reduce new birth to *sozo* alone. They accompany it. They witness to it. They testify that the Kingdom of God is truly at hand and that God is actively bringing a person into a new order of life.

New birth is a miracle, but it is more than a moment of rescue. It is the beginning of a life sourced from above. Saving acts may occur within it - washing, renewal, deliverance, realignment - but new birth itself speaks to origin, capacity, and entry into Kingdom life (John 3:3–5). It is not less than *sozo*. But neither is it merely the same thing.

This is why we must speak carefully. We are not saying that nothing happens in new birth. We are saying that what happens there must not be collapsed into one category alone. The acts of God that attend new birth are real, powerful, and transformative. They are also witnesses: signs that the Fath

Why New Birth Must Be Distinguished from the Saving Act

When new birth is treated as identical with the saving act, several problems quietly emerge.

Rescue language is stretched beyond its purpose. Growth becomes optional. Formation is sidelined. Inheritance is assumed rather than prepared for.

Scripture does not do this.

It speaks of infants, children, and mature sons (First Corinthians 3:1; Hebrews 5:12–14). It distinguishes between milk and solid food (Hebrews 5:12–14). It frames discipline as family life, not punishment (Hebrews 12:5–11).

All of this language assumes that birth precedes development.

Born to Become Something

New birth is not the goal of the gospel.

It is the beginning of God's purpose.

Jesus does not speak of people being born from above so they can remain infants. The New Testament points toward sons who grow, mature, and eventually inherit (Romans 8:14–17; Galatians 4:4–7).

Birth establishes life and identity. Formation shapes character. Sonship prepares for inheritance.

Without birth, none of this is possible. But birth alone does not accomplish it.

What This Reframes for Us

If new birth is not the saving act, then the saving act must be allowed to remain what Scripture presents it to be: God's intervention into threatened life.

And if new birth is about capacity rather than rescue, then the gospel is no longer compressed into a single moment.

It becomes a story with movement.

The saving act clears the threat. Birth grants capacity. Sonship shapes identity. Inheritance awaits maturity.

These are not competing ideas. They are rightly ordered realities.

Where This Leads Next

If new birth grants capacity for Kingdom life, then the next question becomes unavoidable:

What is that life meant to grow into?

Scripture's answer is not vague.

It speaks of sons.

Not merely forgiven people. Not merely rescued people. But sons who bear resemblance, responsibility, and inheritance.

And that is where we turn next.

Scripture Index:

- John 3:3
- John 3:5
- 1 Corinthians 3:1
- Hebrews 5:12–14

- Hebrews 12:5–11
- Romans 8:14–17
- Galatians 4:4–7

Chapter Eight

Sonship: The True Aim of Christ's Work

If the saving act rescues, and new birth grants capacity, then Scripture presses us toward a deeper question:

What was God aiming for all along?

The New Testament's answer is not vague. It does not hesitate. And it does not say merely, the rescued.

It says, sons.

God's Purpose Did Not End with Rescue

Paul does not frame God's purpose merely as a reaction to human failure.

In Romans 8, he reaches beyond the immediate problem of sin and speaks of intention: "*For whom he did foreknow, he also did predestinate to be conformed to the image of his Son, that he might be the firstborn among many brethren*" (Romans 8:29).

This is not merely emergency language. It is family language.

God's saving work addresses what went wrong. Sonship reveals what He was moving toward.

Why Adoption Sits at the Center

Paul's use of adoption is deliberate.

He does not use it merely to describe rescue from danger. He uses it to describe placement into family standing: *"Ye have received the Spirit of adoption, whereby we cry, Abba, Father"* (Romans 8:15). Again, *"God sent forth his Son... that we might receive the adoption of sons"* (Galatians 4:4–5).

Adoption in Paul is not sentimental language. It is purposeful language. Sons are not merely loved; they are brought into inheritance, representation, and responsibility.

This is why Paul ties sonship and adoption to inheritance, suffering, and glory (Romans 8:17).

Adoption is not a decorative metaphor. It is part of the framework of inheritance.

Servants Are Faithful - Sons Are Entrusted

Scripture honors servants.

They obey. They work. They are faithful.

But Scripture also distinguishes servant language from son language. Jesus says, *"And the servant abideth not in the house for ever: but the Son abideth ever"* (John 8:35).

This is not about worth. It is about role and permanence.

The saving act restores a person from threat. Sonship entrusts a person with family responsibility.

God does not speak of inheritance merely in terms of those who were rescued. He speaks of it in the language of children and heirs (Romans 8:14–17; Galatians 4:6–7).

Why Sonship Requires Formation

Here is where clarity matters.

Birth brings a person into life. Sonship brings that life into family order. Inheritance is entered in maturity.

Paul uses an image that would have been unmistakable to his readers: *"Now I say, That the heir, as long as he is a child, differeth nothing from a servant, though he be lord of all"* (Galatians 4:1).

The heir already possesses everything in promise. But access and administration are held under the Father's ordering until the appointed time (Galatians 4:2).

This is not punishment. It is preparation.

Formation - properly understood - is how sons grow into the capacity required for what is already theirs in promise.

Christ's Work Aimed Beyond Forgiveness

The cross accomplishes many things.

It confronts sin. It breaks death. It reconciles humanity to God.

But the New Testament does not stop there.

It points beyond pardon toward family. *"For it became him... in bringing many sons unto glory, to make the captain of their salvation perfect through sufferings"* (Hebrews 2:10).

If forgiveness were the whole horizon, then pardon alone would be sufficient. But if sonship is central to God's purpose, then new birth, formation, discipline, maturity, and inheritance all belong to the same story.

Nothing here diminishes the broader biblical reality we call salvation. It shows the direction of God's saving work.

Why This Changes How We Read the Gospel

When sonship is restored to the center, several things realign.

Discipleship is no longer optional. Obedience is no longer suspect. Discipline is no longer merely punitive. Growth is no longer confused with earning.

These become family realities.

"The Lord loveth he chasteneth" and disciplines sons because He is preparing them, not rejecting them (Hebrews 12:5–11).

The Father does not train sons to test whether they belong. He trains them because they do.

The Firstborn Among Many Brethren

Jesus is not called Firstborn because He was created first.

He is Firstborn because He is the pattern and preeminent Son within the family God is forming (Romans 8:29; Colossians 1:18).

What He is by nature, sons are being prepared to reflect by participation - not equal in essence, but conformed in likeness, purpose, and inheritance.

This is why Scripture ties sonship to glory. This is why suffering and discipline are not meaningless interruptions. This is why inheritance waits for maturity.

God is forming a family capable of sharing His reign.

What Sonship Requires

Sonship is not a title to claim and leave untouched. It is a life to be formed in.

It assumes obedience learned, character shaped, authority restrained, and trust proven.

Not to earn belonging - but because belonging has already been granted, and family likeness must grow where family life is real.

Where This Leads

If sonship is the true aim of Christ's work, then the Christian life cannot be reduced to maintenance.

It is preparation.

The saving act rescues from threat. New birth grants capacity. Sonship shapes family identity and readiness. Inheritance awaits maturity.

And that path - the path of a son - is where we turn next.

Scripture Index:

- Romans 8:29
- Romans 8:15
- Galatians 4:4–5
- Romans 8:17
- John 8:35
- Romans 8:14–17
- Galatians 4:6–7
- Galatians 4:1
- Galatians 4:2
- Hebrews 2:10
- Hebrews 12:5–11
- Colossians 1:18

Chapter Nine

The Path of a Son

Sonship is not static.

It is lived.

Once Scripture restores sonship to the center, it immediately raises a practical question—one that cannot be answered with slogans or shortcuts:

What does the life of a son actually look like?

The New Testament does not leave us guessing. It sketches a path - not a formula, not a ladder, not a checklist, but a trajectory that moves from birth toward inheritance.

From Birth to Identity

Every path begins with birth.

New birth introduces life, but that life must be recognized before it can be lived. This is why Scripture speaks so often of identity - not as self-affirmation, but as orientation. *"Ye are all the children of God by faith in Christ Jesus"* (Galatians 3:26). *"Because ye are sons, God hath sent forth the Spirit of his Son into your hearts, crying, Abba, Father"* (Galatians 4:6). *"Beloved, now are we the sons of God"* (First John 3:2).

These declarations are not goals to reach. They are truths to stand in.

Identity precedes behavior. Belonging precedes obedience.

A son does not learn who he is by performing well. He learns how to live because he knows whose he is.

From Identity to Formation

Once identity is established, growth becomes possible.

This is where many misunderstandings arise.

Growth is not about earning standing. It is about learning function.

Scripture consistently frames this stage as training. Hebrews speaks of discipline not as rejection, but as the Father's treatment of sons (Hebrews 12:5–11). Paul speaks of renewal not as self-improvement, but as transformation shaped by truth: *"be ye transformed by the renewing of your mind"* (Romans 12:2). He also speaks of putting off the old man and putting on the new (Ephesians 4:22–24).

This is family work.

A father trains a son because the son will one day carry weight. Authority without preparation is dangerous. Inheritance without maturity is destructive.

Formation - rightly understood - is the shaping of capacity in those who already belong.

From Formation to Maturity

Maturity is not perfection.

It is stability.

Scripture contrasts children who are easily carried about with those who have grown into discernment (Ephesians 4:13–15). It speaks of those *"who by reason of use have their senses exercised to discern both good and evil"* (Hebrews 5:14). It speaks of minds renewed (Romans 12:2) and hearts established (Hebrews 13:9).

Maturity is the ability to carry responsibility without being ruled by impulse, fear, or immaturity.

It does not arrive all at once.

It is recognized over time.

And it is always relational.

From Maturity to Authority

Authority in Scripture is never seized. It is entrusted.

Jesus does not hand responsibility to the unformed simply because they are eager. Scripture consistently joins entrustment to faithfulness. *"He that is faithful in that which is least is faithful also in much"* (Luke 16:10). *"Well done, thou good and faithful servant: thou hast been faithful over a few things, I will make thee ruler over many things"* (Matthew 25:21). The faithful steward is the one set over the household (Luke 12:42–44).

A son who cannot govern himself cannot govern well for others. A son who has not learned obedience cannot be trusted with power.

This is not harsh. It is merciful.

God does not withhold authority to diminish sons. He withholds it to protect them - and those they would otherwise harm before they are ready.

From Authority to Inheritance

Inheritance is not merely something received at the end.

It is something one must be prepared to carry.

Scripture ties inheritance to sonship, resurrection, and shared reign. "*If children, then heirs*" (Romans 8:17). Creation itself waits for the revealing of the sons of God, and the inheritance ahead is bound up with resurrection life and glory (Romans 8:19, 23). John says that the redeemed "*shall reign on the earth*" (Revelation 5:10). Paul says, "*If we suffer, we shall also reign with him*" (2 Timothy 2:12).

These are not decorative ideas. They are future realities that require present preparation.

The path of a son leads somewhere.

Not to escape. Not to maintenance. But to participation.

Why This Path Is Often Missed

Much of modern Christianity emphasizes beginnings.

Decision. Conversion. Assurance.

Beginnings matter. But when beginnings are mistaken for destinations, growth stalls. And when growth stalls, inheritance fades from view.

The gospel becomes something to protect instead of a life to be lived.

A Path, Not a Pressure

This path is not meant to burden.

It is meant to orient.

Every son walks it differently. Every season shapes something specific. Every delay serves a purpose.

There is no competition here. No comparison. No artificial timeline to meet.

Only a Father who knows what He is preparing His sons for.

What This Clarifies

The Christian life is not aimless.

It is directional.

New birth grants life and Kingdom capacity. Identity anchors belonging. Formation shapes readiness. Maturity stabilizes character. Authority is entrusted. Inheritance awaits.

This is not a system imposed on Scripture.

It is the story Scripture has been telling all along.

Where the Path Ends

If the path of a son moves toward inheritance, then we must finally ask what inheritance actually is - and why Scripture treats it with such gravity.

That question cannot be answered lightly.

And it cannot be skipped.

So we turn, at last, to the endgame Scripture never forgot - even when we did.

Scripture Index:

- Galatians 3:26
- Galatians 4:6
- 1 John 3:2
- Hebrews 12:5–11
- Romans 12:2
- Ephesians 4:22–24
- Ephesians 4:13–15
- Hebrews 5:14
- Hebrews 13:9
- Luke 16:10
- Matthew 25:21
- Luke 12:42–44
- Romans 8:17
- Romans 8:19
- Romans 8:23
- Revelation 5:10
- 2 Timothy 2:12

Chapter Ten

Inheritance: The Forgotten Endgame of the Gospel

Inheritance is one of the most powerful words in Scripture - and one of the most neglected.

It appears quietly, consistently, and insistently across the New Testament. It is spoken to sons, promised to heirs, tied to resurrection, and bound to the reign of Christ. And yet, for many believers, inheritance has been reduced to a synonym for heaven, or set aside as a distant abstraction with little relevance to present life.

Scripture does not treat it that way.

Inheritance is not a metaphor. It is not a consolation prize. And it is not automatic.

It is the direction toward which the gospel moves.

Why Heirs Reign

When Scripture speaks of inheritance, it speaks of authority as well as possession.

Paul says, *"If children, then heirs; heirs of God, and joint-heirs with Christ"* (Romans 8:17). John says that the redeemed are made *"kings and priests,"* and that they *"shall reign on the earth"* (Revelation 5:10). Later, he speaks again of those who *"shall reign with him"* (Revelation 20:6).

Inheritance in Scripture is active. It involves participation in God's rule, not merely nearness to His presence.

This is why the language of kingship, priesthood, and co-rule appears wherever inheritance is discussed. Heirs are entrusted with responsibility because they share the likeness, character, and maturity of the Firstborn.

Inheritance assumes readiness.

Inheritance Is Tied to Resurrection

One of the most overlooked truths in the New Testament is this: inheritance is consistently tied to resurrection, not merely to death.

Peter speaks of *"an inheritance incorruptible, and undefiled, and that fadeth not away, reserved in heaven"* (First Peter 1:4). Paul speaks of *"the redemption of our body"* as part of what creation itself waits for along with the revealing of the sons of God (Romans 8:19, 23). And he insists that what is mortal must put on immortality (1 Corinthians 15:50–54).

This inheritance is not entered through disembodiment. It is entered through renewed life.

Resurrection is not the epilogue of the gospel. It is the gateway to inheritance.

This is why Scripture places such weight on bodily renewal. The reign to come is not abstract. It requires renewed creation and restored humanity capable of bearing glory without being consumed by it.

The Firstborn Among Many Brethren

Jesus is called Firstborn not because He was created first, but because He is the pattern, the preeminent Son, and the heir (Romans 8:29; Colossians 1:18).

Firstborn language is inheritance language.

What belongs to Him by right is being prepared for many to share by participation - not equality of essence, but unity of likeness, purpose, and inheritance.

The Father is not raising an audience. He is raising a household.

And households have heirs.

Why Inheritance Waits

Inheritance is promised early. It is entered in its fullness later.

This delay is not denial. It is wisdom.

Paul's imagery of heirs under tutors and governors until the appointed time explains what many have misunderstood: *"The heir, as long as he is a child, differeth nothing from a servant, though he be lord of all"* (Galatians 4:1–2). The inheritance is not absent. It is protected until sons are ready to bear it.

Power without formation destroys. Authority without maturity corrupts.

God does not rush inheritance. He prepares heirs.

What We Lost When Inheritance Faded

When inheritance disappeared from the center of the gospel, several things quietly followed.

Hope narrowed to survival. Obedience became suspicious. Discipline felt merely punitive. The future shrank to escape.

The gospel became about securing a destination instead of preparing a people.

But Scripture never aimed so small.

Inheritance Changes the Present

Inheritance is future-oriented, but it reshapes the present.

Those who understand what lies ahead endure suffering differently (Romans 8:18). They receive discipline differently (Hebrews 12:5–11). They approach obedience differently. And they even understand the broader reality of salvation differently, because they recognize that God's saving work is moving somewhere.

They are not striving for approval. They are being prepared for responsibility.

Inheritance gives context to everything that precedes it.

What Inheritance Is Not

Inheritance is not earned. It is not seized. It is not claimed by presumption.

It is received by those who are sons and who are being prepared to carry what is promised.

And preparation does not diminish grace. It honors it.

Grace does not eliminate readiness. It makes readiness meaningful.

The Endgame Scripture Never Forgot

From the beginning, God's purpose has moved toward a family of mature sons, conformed to the image of the Firstborn, sharing in His reign over a restored creation (Romans 8:29; Hebrews 2:10).

The saving act intervenes when destruction threatens. New birth grants life and Kingdom capacity. Sonship shapes family identity. Formation prepares readiness. Inheritance entrusts authority.

This is not speculation. It is the narrative Scripture has been telling all along.

Where This Leaves Us

Inheritance does not make the gospel heavier.

It makes it larger.

It does not reduce the need for the saving act. It explains why God's saving work keeps moving forward. It does not deny heaven. It anchors hope in resurrection and reign. And it does not glorify humanity at God's expense. It glorifies God by revealing what He intends His sons to become.

This is the endgame the gospel has always pointed toward. Not escape. Not maintenance. But participation.

Scripture Index:

- Romans 8:17
- Revelation 5:10
- Revelation 20:6
- First Peter 1:4
- Romans 8:19
- Romans 8:23
- 1 Corinthians 15:50–54
- Romans 8:29
- Colossians 1:18
- Galatians 4:1–2
- Romans 8:18
- Hebrews 12:5–11
- Hebrews 2:10

Part IV

Salvation and the Body of Christ

Up to this point, we have spoken carefully about *sozo* as Scripture often presents it -situational, repeated, and enacted wherever life is threatened. We have seen that *sozo* is not first a status, but a saving act; not a destination, but an intervention. We have followed the movement from rescue to new birth, from new birth to sonship, and from sonship toward inheritance.

But Scripture does not allow God's saving work to remain an individual possession.

From the beginning, what God does to save is aimed at more than isolated persons. It moves toward a people. Indicating that God's saving work is corporate.

The modern gospel often speaks in the language of isolation: my salvation, my faith, my walk. Scripture speaks differently. It speaks of a people, a body, a household, a temple being built together (1 Corinthians 12:12–27; Ephesians 2:19–22).

When God acts to save, He does not merely restore a person to themselves. He also restores them into right relation with others.

This is where much of our misunderstanding quietly deepens. We have learned to ask whether I am saved, but we rarely ask whether the Body is whole. We have learned to think of healing, deliverance, and restoration as private experiences, rather than as manifestations of a shared life animated by the Spirit.

The New Testament does not support that separation.

And this is also where the language of *sōtēria* begins to press more fully into view. If *sōzo* often names the saving act, *sōtēria* can speak of the broader outcome, condition, and horizon of God's saving work - presently tasted, corporately lived, and still moving toward future unveiling (Romans 13:11; 1 Peter 1:5, 9; Hebrews 9:28). In Part IV, that broader horizon becomes harder to ignore, because Scripture begins to speak not only of acts of rescue, but of a people being gathered, ordered, strengthened, and prepared together.

Paul speaks of God's saving work in ways that are unmistakably communal.

He warns that failure to discern the Body results not only in division, but in weakness, sickness, and even death (1 Corinthians 11:29–30). He does not frame this merely as punishment. He frames it as consequence - what happens when the life of the Body is misunderstood and misaligned.

In this light, God's saving work is not merely something that happens to individuals, but something He does among a people. It is something that happens within a living organism.

When the Body functions rightly, life flows. When it is fractured, life is impeded.

This section turns our attention to a dimension of God's saving work that modern theology has often neglected: saving acts expressed as shared life, and *sōtēria* as a corporate horizon.

We will explore how *sōzō* operates within the Body of Christ - not as a collection of private miracles, but as expressions of corporate wholeness. We will look again at communion, not as ritual alone, but as discernment of the Body. And we will consider why misunderstanding this reality has tangible effects on health, unity, and spiritual vitality.

We will also examine the gifts of the Spirit, not as badges of spirituality or tools for individual empowerment, but as saving acts distributed through the Body. Healing, deliverance, restoration, prophecy - these are not spiritual accessories. They are the Spirit's way of distributing the life of the Kingdom among the members of Christ (1 Corinthians 12:7–11).

And the Spirit Himself is given not merely as a private comfort, but as *"the earnest of our inheritance"* (Ephesians 1:13–14) - not poured out upon isolated individuals alone, but upon a people being prepared together for what is to come.

Part IV asks us to lift our eyes.

The saving act does not end with the individual. And the broader salvation-horizon of *sōtēria* is not merely personal. God's saving work binds lives together. It restores communion not only with God, but with one another. It gathers a people in the present, prepares them for inheritance in the future, and secures them in the purpose of God.

If the gospel is preparing sons for inheritance, then it must also be forming a Body capable of sharing that inheritance together.

That is where we turn now - not to a new subject, but to a fuller vision of the same saving work at work among a people.

Scripture Index:

- 1 Corinthians 12:12–27
- Ephesians 2:19–22
- Romans 13:11
- 1 Peter 1:5
- 1 Peter 1:9
- Hebrews 9:28
- 1 Corinthians 11:29–30
- 1 Corinthians 12:7–11
- Ephesians 1:13–14

Chapter Eleven

How Sōtēria Relates to the Body, Not Merely the Individual

The New Testament does not treat God's saving work as merely a private possession.

That may sound unfamiliar to modern ears, but it is unmistakable in the text. Saving acts happen to persons, but they are constantly oriented toward a people. The language of Scripture repeatedly pulls us out of isolation and places us into something living, shared, and interconnected.

God's saving work, in its fuller expression, forms a Body.

And this is where the broader horizon of *sōtēria* presses into view again. If *sozo* often names the saving act, *sōtēria* can also speak of the larger condition and outcome of that saving work as it gathers, orders, and prepares a people together. In this chapter, we are not leaving *sozo* behind. We are seeing how saving acts belong within a corporate life.

A Body, Not a Collection

Paul does not describe the church as a gathering of saved individuals who happen to share beliefs. He calls it a body - one life expressed through many members (1 Corinthians 12:12–27). Each member is distinct, but none exist independently.

This matters because bodies do not function on isolated merit. When one part suffers, all suffer with it. When one part is honored, all rejoice with it (1 Corinthians 12:26). Life flows - or is restricted - based on how the whole functions together.

God's saving acts, then, cannot be reduced to what happens in private moments between God and a single believer. They must also be understood as acts that belong within shared life.

Why Paul's Warning Is So Severe

Nowhere is this clearer than in Paul's words to the Corinthians.

They were gathering for the Lord's Supper - an act meant to proclaim unity, shared life, and participation in Christ. But Paul says something startling: because they failed to discern the Body, many among them were weak, sick, and some had even died (1 Corinthians 11:29–30).

This is not the language of mere symbolism. It is not metaphor. And Paul does not frame it first as spectacle or superstition.

He says the Body was misunderstood.

The consequence of that misunderstanding was broken life.

Discerning the Body

To discern the Body is not merely to recognize a doctrine.

It is to understand what kind of reality the church actually is.

The Body of Christ is not an idea. It is a living organism animated by the Spirit. *"By one Spirit are we all baptized into one body"* (1 Corinthians 12:13). The church is also spoken of as a household and a holy temple being built together (Ephesians 2:19–22).

When believers treat one another as separate units - divided by pride, neglect, rivalry, status, or indifference - the Body fractures. And when the Body fractures, the life it carries does not move freely.

Weakness follows. Sickness follows. Life is diminished.

Not because God has ceased to be generous, but because the conditions necessary for shared life are being violated.

Communion as Participation, Not Ritual

This is why communion carries such weight in Scripture.

It is not merely a private moment of reflection. It is not a symbolic reenactment performed in isolation.

It is participation. *"The cup of blessing which we bless, is it not the communion of the blood of Christ? The bread which we break, is it not the communion of the body of Christ?"* (1 Corinthians 10:16). "For we being many are one bread, and one body" (1 Corinthians 10:17).

To partake of the bread and cup is to declare alignment with the Body - to affirm shared dependence, shared life, and shared responsibility. When that declaration is contradicted by how the Body is actually treated, the act becomes dissonant.

Paul's warning is not meant to produce terror. It is meant to restore coherence.

Communion exposes how seriously God takes shared life.

The Life of the Kingdom Saves Where It Flows

When God's saving work is understood corporately, many things come back into focus.

Healing is no longer a private entitlement. Deliverance is no longer a personal spectacle. Restoration is no longer an isolated miracle.

They are expressions of life moving through the Body as it should.

God's saving work is expressed, and acts of *sozo* are manifested where the Body functions in alignment - where members care for one another, honor one another, and recognize that life is shared. This does not mean the saving act belongs to one gifted individual, as though the life of Christ were concentrated in a single leader. Scripture presents something far larger: the whole Body of Christ, congregationally, regionally, and ultimately as one people under one Head, being joined and nourished together (Ephesians 4:15–16; Colossians 2:19).

This is why leadership matters so much. Leaders are not meant to absorb the Body into themselves, but to serve its alignment under Christ. When leadership mistakes headship for control, or visibility for centrality, the Body is often taught dependence where Scripture intended participation.

This does not eliminate individual faith. It situates it.

Faith becomes participatory rather than possessive.

Why Individualism Impedes Wholeness

Modern Christianity often emphasizes personal salvation while neglecting communal discernment.

We ask whether I am healed, whether I am delivered, whether I am whole - without asking whether the Body is functioning rightly.

Scripture does not separate these questions.

A fractured Body cannot sustain shared life well. A misaligned Body cannot mediate healing well. A disconnected people cannot fully display the life they have been given.

This is not mystical exaggeration. It is relational reality.

A Healthier Way Forward

Paul's words are not meant to condemn the church.

They are meant to heal it.

When the Body is discerned rightly - when unity is not theoretical but practiced - God's saving work flows more freely.

Weakness is addressed. Healing becomes less strange. Life is strengthened.

Not through formulas. Not through performance. But through restored communion, shared participation, and proper alignment under Christ the Head.

This is where the broader horizon of *sōtēria* becomes visible again: not only in individual acts of rescue, but in a people being preserved, strengthened, and prepared together for what is to come.

What This Prepares Us For

If *sozo* operates within the Body, then the Spirit's activity among believers must also be understood corporately.

Healing, prophecy, deliverance, restoration - these are not personal trophies. They are saving acts distributed through the Body for the good of all (1 Corinthians 12:7–11).

And the Spirit who animates this shared life is not merely a present helper. He is also *"the earnest of our inheritance"* (Ephesians 1:13–14), the pledge of what the Body will one day inherit together.

That is where we turn next.

Scripture Index:

- Ephesians 2:19–22
- 1 Corinthians 10:16
- 1 Corinthians 10:17
- Ephesians 4:15–16
- Colossians 2:19
- 1 Corinthians 12:7–11
- Ephesians 1:13–14

Chapter Twelve

The Gifts of the Spirit as Saving Acts, and the Fruit That

Governs Them

When the New Testament speaks of the Spirit, it does not speak of ornamentation.

The Spirit is not given to decorate faith, to distinguish the especially spiritual, or to create hierarchies within the church. It is given because God's saving work is still being expressed in the Body, and the Body requires life to flow through it.

The gifts of the Spirit are not spiritual accessories. They are distributed acts through which God's saving work is expressed among His people.

The Spirit Is Given Because God's Purpose Continues

When Jesus said, *"It is finished"* (John 19:30), He was not announcing a failure or deficiency in His work. He was declaring the completion of what He had come to accomplish in His suffering, obedience, and sacrifice.

But the completion of Christ's redemptive work is not the same thing as the completion of God's purpose in a people.

Scripture presents the Spirit as essential - not because Christ's work was unfinished, but because that finished work must still be applied, manifested, and carried through a Body being restored, strengthened, aligned, and prepared for inheritance.

The Spirit does not replace Christ's work. It mediates and applies the life of that work wherever the Body must be healed, ordered, and built up.

It is not given merely to console individuals. It is given because the life of the Kingdom must move through a people.

The Fruit of the Spirit Governs the Gifts of the Spirit

Before speaking further of the gifts of the Spirit, we must say something about the fruit of the Spirit.

The New Testament does not present the Spirit merely as a distributor of manifestations. He is also the One who forms the life of Christ within a people. Paul speaks of *"the fruit of the Spirit"* as love, joy, peace, longsuffering, gentleness, goodness, faith, meekness, and temperance (Galatians 5:22–23). This is not ornamentation. It is evidence that the life of the Spirit is taking proper shape in those through whom He works.

The gifts of the Spirit reveal what the Spirit does through the Body. The fruit of the Spirit reveals what the Spirit is forming within the members of that Body. Gifts express function. Fruit reveals character. Gifts distribute power. Fruit governs its use.

This is why Paul's sequence matters. He speaks of gifts in 1 Corinthians 12, places love at the center in 1 Corinthians 13, and then returns to the ordered use of gifts in 1 Corinthians 14. A people may be gifted and still be immature. They may manifest power and still wound the Body if love, humility, patience, and self-restraint are absent. Fruit does not make the gifts unnecessary. It makes them trustworthy.

This matters deeply for the argument of this chapter. If the gifts are distributed acts through which God's saving work is expressed in the Body, then fruit is one of the clearest indicators that the Body is functioning rightly. Where the fruit of the Spirit is neglected, the gifts are easily turned into performance, hierarchy, or spectacle. But where love governs, peace steadies, patience restrains, and self-control matures, the gifts become what they were always meant to be: edifying acts of life flowing through the Body for the good of all.

Healing: A Saving Act Confronting Broken Flesh

Healing is one of the clearest expressions of *sozo* in Scripture.

When the Spirit heals, He is not merely performing a sign to confirm doctrine. He is confronting what threatens life in the Body. Healing restores function, not only to individuals, but to the community that depends on them.

A healed member strengthens the whole Body. An untreated wound weakens it.

Healing is a saving act where sickness threatens shared life.

Deliverance: A Saving Act Breaking Bondage

Deliverance is often misunderstood because it exposes realities many would prefer to keep abstract.

Scripture does not hesitate.

Where bondage exists, God acts to save. Where oppression limits life, the Spirit acts.

Deliverance is not about sensationalism or blame. It is about restoring agency, clarity, and peace to members of the Body so that life can move freely again.

This is not power for display. It is a saving act restoring function.

Restoration: A Saving Act Repairing What Was Fractured

Some damage is not dramatic. It is slow, relational, and cumulative.

Broken trust. Lingering shame. Wounded conscience. Dislocated fellowship.

The Spirit restores where life has worn down. He repairs relationships, reestablishes belonging, and brings coherence where fragmentation has taken root.

Restoration is not a performance of spirituality. It is the reappearance of life where life has been diminished.

Prophecy: A Saving Act Revealing Truth in Real Time

Prophecy is often reduced to prediction.

Scripture frames it differently.

Prophecy reveals what God is saying and doing now. It brings alignment, clarity, correction, and encouragement. Properly exercised, prophecy strengthens the Body by exposing what threatens life and affirming what sustains it.

Paul says that the one who prophesies speaks "unto men to edification, and exhortation, and comfort" (1 Corinthians 14:3). In that sense, prophecy rescues understanding from confusion and direction from drift.

This too belongs to the pattern of God's saving work.

Why the Gifts Belong to the Body

The Spirit does not distribute gifts according to personal worth.

He distributes them according to need and for the common good (1 Corinthians 12:7–11).

This alone should end competition.

No gift exists for its own sake. No gift exists for self-identification. No gift exists apart from the Body.

Each manifestation is a distributed expression of God's saving work where it is required.

One of the quiet distortions in modern discussions of spiritual gifts is the assumption that the gift belongs to the one through whom it operates. Scripture does not support this. The gift of healing, for instance, is not given for the exaltation of the one who prays, but for the good of the one who is threatened and the Body to which that person belongs. The obedient servant is not the point. The life of Christ moving through the Body is the point.

Over time, some believers become more sensitive to when and how the Spirit intends to act. That sensitivity is not a badge of honor. It is not ownership. It is maturity. It develops the same way all maturity does - through obedience, restraint, and familiarity with the ways of God. Even where Scripture speaks of particular operations being associated with particular people, the purpose is never personal elevation. The gifts exist to edify the Body, not to magnify the individual.

This is why certain gifts make no sense apart from the Body. Interpretation of tongues, for example, has no value if it terminates in the individual. The message is not complete when it is merely experienced; it is complete when the Body is edified.

The Spirit as the Earnest of the Inheritance

Paul calls the Spirit *"the earnest of our inheritance"* (Ephesians 1:13–14) - the down payment of what is to come.

This means the Spirit's present work is not random. It previews the future.

Healing anticipates resurrection. Deliverance anticipates freedom. Restoration anticipates wholeness. Prophecy anticipates ordered life under God's reign.

The Spirit is not preparing isolated individuals for heaven. He is preparing a Body for inheritance.

And this is where the broader horizon of *sōtēria* becomes visible again: not only in individual acts of rescue, but in a people being preserved, strengthened, ordered, and prepared together for what is to come.

What We Missed When the Gifts Were Misframed

When the gifts were turned into proofs of spirituality, they lost their purpose.

When they were rejected as unnecessary, God's saving work was narrowed. When they were commodified, the Body was fractured.

Scripture gives us permission neither to idolize nor to dismiss them.

It calls us to discern them.

A Mature Use of the Spirit's Work

The goal is not more manifestations.

The goal is more life.

Where the Spirit is welcomed rightly, God's saving work is expressed more freely through the Body. Where the Body is honored, gifts function more naturally. Where inheritance is kept in view, the Spirit's work remains grounded. Where servant leadership is broken, and where the Body is bent around human control rather than Christ its Head, the gifts are easily distorted or impeded.

The gifts do not replace the gospel, nor do they exhaust God's saving work. They are distributed acts through which that saving work is expressed in the Body.

Where This Leaves the Body

God's saving work does not end at the cross, nor at conversion, nor in private experience alone.

It continues wherever the Spirit moves life through the Body.

And the Spirit who heals, restores, and reveals today is the same Spirit preparing a people for what lies ahead.

This is God's saving work at work - not as spectacle, but as shared life moving toward inheritance.

Scripture Index:

- Galatians 5:22–23
- 1 Corinthians 12
- 1 Corinthians 13
- 1 Corinthians 14
- 1 Corinthians 14:3
- 1 Corinthians 12:7–11
  Ephesians 1:13–14

Part V

The Gospel Jesus Actually Preached

By this point, much of what we have inherited as "the gospel" should feel familiar - and yet incomplete.

Not false in every respect. But reduced.

Throughout this book, we have tried to follow Scripture's own language carefully. We have resisted the urge to collapse distinct realities into inherited formulas, or to force the text to answer questions it was not always asking. And as we have done so, a quiet realization has emerged:

Jesus did not preach the gospel we learned to summarize.

He preached the gospel of the Kingdom (Mark 1:14–15; Matthew 4:17).

The Gospels do not record Jesus traveling from town to town explaining how to get saved in the modern reduced sense. They do not present Him offering a message centered on escaping hell or securing a future destination. Instead, they repeatedly show Him announcing something far more immediate and far more demanding:

"The kingdom of God is at hand" (Mark 1:15).

That announcement was not theoretical. It was not postponed. And it was not merely personal.

It was an invitation into a reign already arriving, a rule already pressing into the present, and a life that required Response.

And the works of Jesus were not detached from that announcement. They bore witness to it. *"The works which the Father hath given me to finish, the same works that I do, bear witness of me"* (John 5:36). When demons were cast out, when bodies were healed, when lives were restored, these were not side notes to the message. They were signs that the Kingdom had truly drawn near (Matthew 12:28).

When Jesus called people to repent, He was not merely asking them to feel sorry in order to qualify for forgiveness. He was calling them to reorient their allegiance - to turn from rival kingdoms and align themselves with God's reign.

When He called people to believe, He was not asking them merely to assent to propositions. He was calling them to trust the announcement that God's Kingdom was breaking in through Him.

And when people were baptized, it was not a bare symbol of something already finished in every sense, nor a mechanical rite detached from faith and obedience. It was a real act of cleansing, transition, incorporation, and entry into a new order of life under the reign of God (Acts 2:38; Acts 22:16; Romans 6:3–4; 1 Peter 3:21). It was not a formula for private assurance. It was part of the way into Kingdom life.

The gospel Jesus preached was not about creating forgiven individuals waiting for heaven.

It was about forming a people - sons and daughters - who would live under God's rule now and be prepared to share in it fully later.

This is why Jesus spoke constantly of authority, obedience, stewardship, fruitfulness, and inheritance (Matthew 28:18–20; Luke 12:42–44; John 15:8, 16; Matthew 25:21). And it is why He so often spoke in the language of a Father, a household, sons, and a Kingdom (Matthew 6:9–10; John 8:35; Luke 12:32).

Part V brings us back to the beginning.

Not to undo what has been said, but to see it whole.

We will look again at the gospel Jesus proclaimed—not as a competing message to God's saving work, but as the context that gives that saving work its meaning. We will examine repentance, belief, and baptism not as isolated steps, but as Responses to the nearness of God's Kingdom. And we will return to the question Scripture never abandons:

What did Jesus come to restore?

The answer is not smaller than what we have been taught.

It is larger.

And it centers not on escape, but on sons revealed in glory under a reigning King.

That is the gospel Jesus preached.

And it is where we now turn.

Scripture Index:

- Mark 1:14–15
- Matthew 4:17
- Mark 1:15
- John 5:36
- Matthew 12:28
- Acts 2:38
- Acts 22:16
- Romans 6:3–4
- 1 Peter 3:21
- Matthew 28:18–20
- Luke 12:42–44
- John 15:8
- John 15:16
- Matthew 25:21
- Matthew 6:9–10
- John 8:35
- Luke 12:32

Chapter Thirteen

The Gospel of the Kingdom

If we listen carefully to Jesus, one thing becomes immediately clear:

He did not preach a message centered on how to get saved in the modern reduced sense.

That statement may sound unsettling, but it is simply textual. The Gospel writers are remarkably consistent in how they summarize Jesus' message, and they do not use the language we later learned to prioritize. They tell us again and again what He proclaimed - and they use the same Kingdom language repeatedly.

Jesus preached the gospel of the Kingdom of God.

What Jesus Actually Announced

The earliest summary of Jesus' ministry is brief and unmistakable:

"Jesus came into Galilee, preaching the gospel of the kingdom of God, and saying, The time is fulfilled, and the kingdom of God is at hand: repent ye, and believe the gospel" (Mark 1:14–15; see also Matthew 4:17, 23).

This announcement is not framed around individual destiny. It is framed around divine reign.

The Kingdom is not described as distant. It is not postponed. It is not internalized into abstraction.

It is at hand.

That phrase alone tells us what kind of message Jesus was preaching. He was not offering information about a future escape. He was announcing that God's rule was breaking into the present and demanding Response.

Why the Kingdom Is Not "How to Get Saved"

The gospel Jesus preached does not answer the question, *How do I get saved?* - at least not in the reduced modern sense that makes rescue the whole headline.

It answers a different question:

Who is King, and what does that mean for my life?

The language of being saved appears within that announcement, but it is never the headline. When people are healed, delivered, restored, or forgiven in the Gospels, those moments are not presented as the gospel itself. They are signs that the Kingdom is present and active.

And more than signs, they are witnesses. Jesus says, *"The works which the Father hath given me to finish, the same works that I do, bear witness of me"* (John 5:36). When demons are cast out, Jesus says, "the kingdom of God is come unto you" (Matthew 12:28).

The saving acts do not define the Kingdom. The Kingdom explains the saving acts.

That order matters.

Why the Kingdom Is Not "How to Get to Heaven"

Jesus rarely speaks about heaven as a destination in the way later tradition often has.

When He speaks of heaven, it is most often to describe authority, origin, and rule - the source of the Kingdom, not merely the place believers hope to go when they die.

The gospel of the Kingdom is not about leaving earth behind. It is about heaven's reign coming to earth.

This is why Jesus teaches His disciples to pray, "*Thy kingdom come. Thy will be done in earth, as it is in heaven*" (Matthew 6:10).

A gospel centered on departure would not pray this prayer.

Repentance in Kingdom Terms

When Jesus calls people to repent, He is not merely demanding emotional sorrow as an entry fee.

Repentance means reorientation - of mind, perception, and allegiance. In Kingdom terms, repentance is the recognition that another rule has arrived, and that loyalty must shift.

People repented because the Kingdom confronted their assumptions, priorities, and sources of authority.

Repentance was not merely preparation for forgiveness. It was Response to reign.

Belief as Trust in the Announcement

To believe the gospel, as Jesus uses the term, is not merely to assent to a doctrine.

It is to trust the announcement that God's Kingdom is arriving through Him.

Belief aligns a person with the reality being proclaimed. It is confidence that what Jesus says is true - and that it demands obedience.

This is why belief in the Gospels is active. Those who believe follow, obey, and realign their lives (John 8:31; Matthew 4:19).

Belief is not passive acceptance. It is Kingdom allegiance.

The Saving Acts Within the Kingdom

When the language of being saved appears in the Gospels, it is always contextual.

People are saved from sickness, from demons, from death, from exclusion, from shame. These acts of *sozo* do not replace the Kingdom message. They demonstrate it.

Each act of rescue is evidence that the King is present and exercising authority.

The saving act does not define the Kingdom. The Kingdom gives the saving act its meaning.

Why Jesus Spoke of Sons

The gospel of the Kingdom is ultimately about family.

Kings rule, but they also have heirs. Jesus does not gather subjects alone; He gathers sons and daughters. He teaches them to pray to a Father, not merely to submit to a ruler (Matthew 6:9–10). He speaks of the Son abiding in the house (John 8:35). He speaks of a little flock to whom the Father gives the Kingdom (Luke 12:32).

This is why sonship, inheritance, and authority appear so naturally in Jesus' teaching. They are not later theological additions. They are embedded in the Kingdom message itself.

The Kingdom produces sons who share the life, character, and purposes of the King.

What We Lost When the Kingdom Was Reduced

When the gospel of the Kingdom was reduced to a message about personal salvation in the modern narrowed sense, several things faded from view.

Authority became abstract. Obedience became suspect. Discipleship became optional. Inheritance became obscure.

The gospel shrank.

But Jesus never preached a small gospel.

The Gospel in Its Proper Shape

The gospel Jesus preached announces that God's reign has arrived, allegiance must change, life must be reoriented, and a people are being formed under a King.

The saving acts happen within that announcement, not apart from it. Repentance, belief, baptism, healing, deliverance, and restoration all find their place here - not as ends in themselves, but as Responses to a Kingdom that has come near.

This is the gospel in its proper shape.

And it prepares us to ask the next question:

How does one enter this Kingdom?

That is where we turn next.

Scripture Index:

- Mark 1:14–15
- Matthew 4:17
- Matthew 4:23
- John 5:36
- Matthew 12:28
- Matthew 6:10
- John 8:31
- Matthew 4:19
- Matthew 6:9–10
- John 8:35
- Luke 12:32

Chapter Fourteen

Believe, Repent, Be Baptized, and Receive the Spirit: The

Way into the Kingdom

When Jesus announced that the Kingdom of God was at hand, He did not toss men a mystery and walk away.

He did not stand in Galilee scattering riddles into the wind and then leave the crowds to guess how heaven expected them to answer.

The Response was not hidden. The call was clear. The New Testament answer to the nearness of the Kingdom comes into view with unmistakable force: believe, repent, be baptized, and receive the Spirit (Mark 1:15; Acts 2:38).

These are not disconnected religious chores. They are not a checklist for nervous people trying to secure a private future. They are living Responses to the arrival of God's reign.

That is where modern preaching often loses the plot. We took what Scripture keeps together and pulled it apart. We turned belief into agreement, repentance into regret, baptism into either a stage prop or a church fight, and the Spirit into an optional add-on for the especially spiritual.

But Scripture speaks with more weight than that.

The Kingdom is not an idea to admire. It is a reign to enter.

Belief: Receiving the King's Word

Jesus often proclaimed, "*Repent ye, and believe the gospel*" (Mark 1:15). That is the public summons. But inside the heart, no one turns toward a King they do not first believe is speaking truth.

Faith comes by hearing, and hearing by the word of God (Romans 10:17). The Father draws (John 6:44). The word is received. And what is received begins to work on the conscience.

To believe the gospel is not to nod politely at theology. It is to trust that Jesus is telling the truth - that the Kingdom really has drawn near, that the King really has come, and that surrender to Him is not loss but life.

Belief is not passive assent. It is Kingdom allegiance.

It is the difference between standing on the shore saying, "I suppose the river is real," and stepping toward it because you trust the voice calling you there.

This is why belief in Scripture never remains merely theoretical. Those who believe follow. They obey. They reorder their lives under the word of the King. Belief is not admiration. Belief is not theological applause. Belief is trust with weight on it. Trust that leans. Trust that moves.

Repentance: When Rival Rule Breaks

Repentance is the first visible movement, but it is not cold, sterile, or mechanical.

It is not a man sitting in a chair muttering, "I have updated my opinion."

Repentance is the soul turning because truth has cut too deep to keep walking in the same direction.

Paul says godly sorrow produces repentance (2 Corinthians 7:10). That means repentance is not emotional manipulation, and it is not self-hatred dressed up as holiness. It is the ache of clarity. It is what happens when the received word exposes what sin has done, what rebellion has distorted, and what must now change.

Repentance is not merely feeling sorrow, though it is rarely untouched by pain. Light hurts when it first hits eyes that have lived in the dark.

And that pain is mercy.

Repentance does not earn access to the Kingdom. It abandons rival rule. It is the soul saying, "I cannot keep calling this lord when the King has arrived."

That is why repentance in the Gospels is never just inner sorrow. It is reorientation. Mind turning. Heart turning. Allegiance turning. A life beginning to bend toward the reign of God.

Baptism: Where the Response Gets Wet

Then comes baptism.

And this is where modern theology often loses its nerve. Some reduce baptism to symbolism so thin it could disappear in a sentence. Others treat it as a mechanical act that works regardless of faith, repentance, or the authority under which it is entered. The New Testament does neither.

Baptism is not empty. And baptism is not magic.

It is a decisive act of transition. It is where cleansing, burial, separation, and incorporation meet obedience in the water.

Something happens there.

Scripture speaks of sins being washed away (Acts 22:16). It speaks of union with Christ's death and resurrection (Romans 6:3–4). It speaks of putting on Christ (Galatians 3:27). It speaks of being brought into one body (1 Corinthians 12:13). The New Testament does not speak of baptism like a church photo-op with wetter clothes. It speaks of it as participatory, covenantal, and weight-bearing.

That is why baptism cannot be reduced to a private symbol of an inward idea. It is obedience made visible. It is faith with a body. It is trust that finally stopped talking from the shore and stepped into the water.

Not a Bare Symbol - But Not a Mechanical Rite

Here we must speak carefully, because this is where people either flatten baptism or inflate it.

Baptism is never treated in the New Testament as a bare symbol, as though heaven watches politely while nothing actually happens. But neither is it treated as a mechanical guarantee, as though water performs independently of faith, repentance, the blood, the Spirit, and the authority of Christ.

When Scripture explicitly says baptism saves, it says so plainly (1 Peter 3:21). Where it does not say that, we have no right to force the category.

So baptism must be honored without being mechanized.

It is not magic words over water. It is not a ritual machine. It is not heaven's vending system.

It is obedient participation under the authority of the risen Christ.

That is exactly why *Baptized* insisted that Matthew 28:18–20 and Acts 2:38 are not competing formulas but complementary expressions of the same authority. Jesus did not hand out a recital script. Peter did not edit the script. Heaven does not respond to vowels. Heaven responds to covenantal authority under the risen Christ. The blood established the covenant. The Name enforces the covenant. The Spirit witnesses the covenant. And the water stands under that covenant as witness, not as a self-contained source of power (Matthew 28:18–20; Acts 2:38; 1 John 5:8).

Baptism does not complete every category we have discussed in this book. It does not erase the distinctions between saving act, new birth, sonship, and inheritance. But it does stand at the threshold where obedience answers revelation and enters the life of the Kingdom.

It is not the whole story. But it is not scenery.

Receive the Spirit: The Life of the Kingdom Entering the House

The Kingdom answer does not stop at the water.

Peter did not say only, "*Repent, and be baptized.*" He also said, "*and ye shall receive the gift of the Holy Ghost*" (Acts 2:38). The Spirit is not decoration. He is not religious ornamentation. He is not heaven's way of making believers more interesting.

He is the life of the Kingdom entering the house.

This is where the chapter must keep step with Scripture. The Spirit is promised as part of the Kingdom Response, but Acts also shows that heaven is not chained to one rigid choreography. In Samaria, believers were baptized and later received the Spirit through the laying on of hands (Acts 8:12–17). In Caesarea, the Spirit fell before the water, and the water followed in obedience (Acts 10:44–48). In Ephesus, fuller revelation brought believers to the water, and the Spirit came upon them afterward (Acts 19:1–6).

Different sequences. Same Lord. Same Kingdom. Same witness.

So we do not make the Spirit an optional afterthought, and we do not turn the book of Acts into a mechanical chart. The point is not to trap heaven in our order. The point is to see that the Kingdom does not come empty. When men and women believe, repent, are baptized, and receive the Spirit, they are not merely being processed through religious steps. They are being brought into the life of a new order.

The Spirit is the gift of the Kingdom present now - and the earnest of what is still to come.

Why Expectancy for Baptism Has Weakened

Many modern believers no longer expect much to happen in baptism.

And that is not because Scripture is shy. It is because the gospel was narrowed first.

Once everything was reduced to a single private event completed entirely at belief, baptism was almost guaranteed to shrink. It could only become a symbol of what had already happened somewhere else. A badge. A testimony slot. A religious announcement to the audience.

But when the gospel is restored to its Kingdom frame, baptism regains its gravity. It is not a competitor to faith. It is faith embodied. It is trust expressed through obedience. It is the body saying yes to what the heart has begun to confess.

Where baptism is reduced, expectancy disappears. Where expectancy disappears, obedience gets dressed up as ceremony. And where ceremony replaces witness, the river is still there, but men stop expecting heaven to speak around it.

Baptism and the Body

Baptism also does something modern Christianity often forgets: it brings people into a people.

It does not unite a person to Christ in abstraction and then leave them floating in spiritual individualism. It incorporates them into the Body.

That is why baptism in Scripture is never treated as a private spirituality project. It assumes witnesses. It assumes shared life. It assumes belonging. It assumes that the one stepping into the water is not stepping into isolation but into Kingdom community.

One does not enter the Kingdom alone.

One may come trembling. One may come uncertain. One may come with only enough light to obey the next step. But no one is baptized into solitude.

The river is not merely about me and Jesus. It is about the King and His people. It is about belonging, alignment, accountability, nourishment, and life flowing in a body that is bigger than one man's experience.

A Way, Not a Formula

Believe, repent, be baptized, and receive the Spirit are not items on a doctrinal punch card.

They are coordinated Responses to one reality: the arrival of God's reign.

Belief receives the King's word. Repentance realigns allegiance. Baptism enacts the transition into Kingdom life and Kingdom community. The Spirit brings the life of that Kingdom into the believer and the Body.

Together, they form the way into the Kingdom—not a formula for securing private reassurance, but the living answer Scripture gives to the nearness of God's reign.

And this matters because formulas are always trying to do what only relationship can do.

Religion loves formulas because formulas can be managed. The Kingdom gives commands instead. And commands require surrender.

Holding the Tension Faithfully

The New Testament never collapses these Responses into one flat idea. But neither does it let us tear them apart into unrelated acts.

It holds them together - distinct, ordered, alive.

When we do the same, belief regains its weight. Repentance regains its ache. Baptism regains its expectancy. And receiving the Spirit regains its place as the life of the Kingdom, not a marginal doctrine for a few enthusiasts.

Then the way into the Kingdom begins to sound less like a denominational argument and more like what it always was: a King calling men and women out of old rule and into a new order of life.

Where This Leads

If the gospel Jesus preached was the gospel of the Kingdom, then belief, repentance, baptism, and receiving the Spirit were never the destination.

They were the beginning.

They are the doorway, not the house. The threshold, not the inheritance. The first yes, not the whole song.

But beginnings matter. And when the beginning is answered rightly, the road ahead opens with far more clarity.

The King did not come merely to gather forgiven people. He came to restore what was lost, reveal sons, and prepare a people for His reign.

And that is where the story now turns.

Scripture Index:

- Mark 1:15
- Acts 2:38
- Romans 10:17
- John 6:44
- 2 Corinthians 7:10
- Acts 22:16
- Romans 6:3–4
- Galatians 3:27
- 1 Corinthians 12:13
- 1 Peter 3:21

- Matthew 28:18–20
- 1 John 5:8
- Acts 8:12–17
- Acts 10:44–48
- Acts 19:1–6

Chapter Fifteen

The King and His Sons

If the gospel Jesus preached was the gospel of the Kingdom, then it necessarily leads us to a final, unavoidable question:

What kind of Kingdom is this - and who is meant to rule within it?

The New Testament's answer is not abstract. It is familial.

Jesus came proclaiming a King, but He came forming sons.

And that language must be handled carefully. The rule Scripture speaks of is not the rise of religious strongmen, nor the sanctifying of human control in the house of God. It is the restoration of a people under the reign of the Son, conformed to His image, and prepared to share in His rule under Him and with Him (Romans 8:14–17, 29; Revelation 5:10).

What Jesus Came to Restore

From the opening pages of Scripture, humanity is presented with a calling.

Dominion was given. Authority was entrusted. Responsibility followed. God said, *"Let us make man in our image, after our likeness: and let them have dominion"* (Genesis 1:26–28).

Humanity was not created merely to exist. Humanity was created to image God and to rule under Him.

The tragedy of the fall was not merely moral failure. It was the fracturing of vocation. Humanity did not cease to exist; it ceased to rule rightly. Dominion was distorted. Authority was bent out of shape. Relationship with God collapsed into fear and hiding (Genesis 3:8–10).

This is why the temptation of Jesus matters so much. Satan showed Him *"all the kingdoms of the world"* and said, *"All this power will I give thee... for that is delivered unto me"* (Luke 4:5–6). What the tempter offered was not random. It was dominion in corrupted form - the rule humanity had failed to guard and now encountered in alien hands.

Jesus did not come simply to fix behavior.

He came to restore rule.

Not rule apart from God - but rule under Him, in His image, by His life, and under His King.

The Kingdom Requires Sons

A Kingdom cannot be sustained by servants alone.

Servants obey. Sons inherit.

Jesus speaks in these terms repeatedly - not to diminish obedience, but to explain destiny. *"The servant abideth not in the house for ever: but the Son abideth ever"* (John 8:35). Paul says, *"As many as are led by the Spirit of God, they are the sons of God,"* and then adds, *"if children, then heirs; heirs of God, and joint-heirs with Christ"* (Romans 8:14–17). Again, *"Because ye are sons, God hath sent forth the Spirit of his Son into your hearts"* (Galatians 4:6–7).

This language is not decorative. It is Kingdom architecture.

The King intends not merely to pardon subjects, but to raise sons.

And Scripture does say more than that. Jesus tells the little flock, *"it is your Father's good pleasure to give you the kingdom"* (Luke 12:32). He tells faithful disciples that they will sit in His kingdom (Luke 22:29–30). Revelation speaks of a redeemed people who *"shall reign on the earth"* (Revelation 5:10).

The King intends to share His reign.

But not with the immature, the self-exalting, or the self-appointed.

With sons.

What Shared Reign Actually Looks Like

This is where the chapter must be read with fear and clarity.

To say that Christ shares His reign with His people does **not** mean that Christian leaders become little kings over the house of God. It does **not** mean pastors, prophets, or apostles are free to enthrone themselves over consciences, control lives, or rule by intimidation.

Jesus explicitly forbids that model.

"The kings of the Gentiles exercise lordship over them... but ye shall not be so" (Luke 22:25–26). Again, *"whosoever will be great among you, let him be your minister"* (Matthew 20:25–28).

So what does shared reign actually look like?

Now, it looks like faithful stewardship, self-government under the Spirit, obedience, servanthood, discernment, and entrusted responsibility (Luke 12:42–44; Matthew 25:21). It looks like likeness before authority, service before recognition, and maturity before entrustment.

Later, in its fullness, it looks like resurrection life, inheritance, and participation with Christ in the restored order of creation (Romans 8:17–19; Revelation 20:6; 22:5).

So the ruling language of Scripture is real - but it is never permission for domination within the church.

It is the promise of mature participation under the King.

Why Sonship Matters More Than Status

Much of modern Christianity has focused on status - saved or not saved, in or out, accepted or rejected.

Jesus speaks instead of relationship and responsibility.

Sonship is not a label. It is a role.

A son bears the Father's likeness. A son represents the Father's interests. A son exercises authority in alignment with the Father's will.

This is why sonship requires growth, discipline, and preparation. Authority without likeness is tyranny. Power without maturity destroys.

The Father does not rush sons into rule.

He prepares them for it.

Dominion Lost and Regained

Scripture presents Jesus as the One who succeeds where humanity failed.

He resists temptation where Adam did not (Matthew 4:1–11; compare Genesis 3). He exercises authority rightly. He obeys fully. He does not seize dominion through compromise, nor accept rule on the serpent's terms.

But He does not do this merely as an example.

He does it as the Firstborn.

Paul says that God predestined His people to be *"conformed to the image of his Son, that he might be the firstborn among many brethren"* (Romans 8:29). What He restores in Himself, He intends to share - not independently, not competitively, but corporately, through a people conformed to His image.

Dominion is not seized back through fleshly force.

It is restored through sonship.

The Sons of God Revealed

Paul speaks of a future moment when *"the earnest expectation of the creature waiteth for the manifestation of the sons of God"* (Romans 8:19).

This is not about recognition alone. It is about function.

Creation is not waiting for applause lines, platform ministries, or religious empires. It is waiting for sons who govern as sons, not tyrants - sons who bear the likeness of the Firstborn and therefore rule without corruption.

This unveiling is not disconnected from resurrection, inheritance, or the fullness of the Kingdom. It is the culmination of everything God has been preparing.

Why Glory Follows Sonship

Glory in Scripture is not merely display.

It is weight.

It is the capacity to bear responsibility without corruption, authority without domination, and power without loss of love. Paul says that if we suffer with Him, we shall also be glorified together (Romans 8:17). Hebrews says Christ is *"bringing many sons unto glory"* (Hebrews 2:10).

Sons are revealed in glory because they have been prepared to carry it.

This is why suffering, discipline, and formation appear so consistently in the path Scripture describes. They are not detours. They are preparation (Hebrews 12:5–11).

What This Means for the Gospel

If the end of the story is sons reigning with the King, then the gospel cannot be reduced to rescue alone.

The saving act intervenes where life is threatened. New birth grants capacity for Kingdom life. Sonship shapes identity and responsibility. Inheritance entrusts authority.

Each has its place.

None replace the others.

The gospel Jesus preached is not smaller than what we inherited.

It is larger.

Where This Leaves Us

The King has come. The Kingdom is at hand. And sons are being prepared.

This does not diminish grace.

It reveals its intention.

God is not merely saving people from destruction. He is restoring a people for faithful participation under His reign - first in likeness, then in stewardship, and finally in glory.

That is what Jesus came to do.

And it is the gospel He never stopped preaching.

Scripture Index:

- Genesis 1:26–28
- Genesis 3:8–10
- Luke 4:5–6
- Romans 8:14–17
- Romans 8:19
- Romans 8:29
- John 8:35
- Galatians 4:6–7
- Luke 12:32
- Luke 22:25–30
- Revelation 5:10
- Luke 12:42–44
- Matthew 20:25–28
- Matthew 25:21
- Revelation 20:6
- Revelation 22:5
- Matthew 4:1–11
- Genesis 3
- Hebrews 2:10
- Romans 8:17
- Hebrews 12:5–11

Part VI

Rewriting the Story of Salvation

By now, the familiar story of salvation should feel different.

Not because Scripture has changed, but because the lens through which we learned to read it has begun to clear.

For many of us, salvation was taught as a finished explanation rather than an ongoing story. We were given answers before we were taught how to read the text. Conclusions before context. A destination before a narrative. Over time, those conclusions hardened into assumptions, and those assumptions quietly began to govern what we could and could not see in Scripture.

This section is not an attempt to move away from the New Testament's message. It is an invitation to bring our reading back into alignment with what the New Testament is actually saying.

Much of modern theology approaches the New Testament with a single controlling question:

How does this tell me how to get to heaven?

But the writers of the New Testament were not organizing their message around that question. They were announcing a Kingdom (Mark 1:14–15). They were describing rescue in many forms. They were forming a people into sons and heirs (Romans

145

8:14–17). They were pointing toward inheritance, glory, and the revealing of the sons of God (Romans 8:19; Hebrews 2:10).

When salvation is reduced to escape, the story shrinks. Texts are flattened. Words are forced to carry meanings they were never intended to bear. And rich, layered language - *sozo*, new birth, adoption, inheritance - is collapsed into a single moment that must explain everything.

This is not how Scripture tells its own story.

Part VI invites us to step back and let the text speak again on its own terms.

We will examine how tradition has trained us to read certain passages reflexively, and how loosening that reflex opens new clarity. We will see that God's saving work appears in Scripture not as a single thin explanation, but as repeated divine intervention wherever life is threatened. We will trace the many ways God saves across a single life without turning the saving act into a process or reducing salvation to a status. And we will also reckon with the broader horizon Scripture gives to salvation - presently tasted, still being approached, and awaiting final unveiling (1 Peter 1:3–5, 9; Romans 13:11).

And finally, we will confront a quiet but decisive shift that occurred in the Church's telling of the gospel: the movement from salvation as preparation for becoming, to salvation as permission to escape.

This section does not ask you to abandon what you believe God has done in you.

It asks you to let that work find its proper place in a larger story.

A story where the saving act intervenes, new birth enables, sonship matures, and inheritance awaits.

Salvation was never meant to be the end of the story.

It was meant to open it.

That is the story we now return to - not to rewrite Scripture, but to relearn how to tell it in the language and order Scripture itself gives.

Scripture Index:

- Mark 1:14–15
- Romans 8:14–17
- Romans 8:19
- Hebrews 2:10
- 1 Peter 1:3–5
- 1 Peter 1:9
- Romans 13:11

Chapter Sixteen

How to Read the New Testament Without Tradition

Every reader comes to Scripture wearing lenses.

Some are inherited from sermons. Some from study Bibles. Some from altar calls, youth camps, or well-meaning teachers who handed us conclusions before they handed us tools.

Tradition is not the enemy of Scripture. But tradition becomes dangerous when it decides, in advance, what the text is allowed to say. Jesus warned that tradition can make *"the word of God of none effect"* (Mark 7:13).

This chapter is not about suspicion.

It is about attention.

The Lens We Rarely Question

For many believers, one assumption quietly governs the entire New Testament:

Salvation means going to heaven when you die.

That assumption is so familiar that it feels self-evident. Verses are read through it automatically. Words like "saved," "life," "kingdom," and "inheritance" are flattened into a single idea: escape.

But familiarity is not the same as faithfulness.

When we bring that lens to the text, we do not really read Scripture. We translate it prematurely.

Jesus announced that *"the kingdom of God is at hand"* (Mark 1:14–15). He told Nicodemus that a man must be born again to see the Kingdom and born of water and Spirit to enter it (John 3:3–5). Paul spoke not merely of the rescued, but of sons, heirs, and joint-heirs with Christ (Romans 8:14–17). Those are not small shifts in vocabulary. They are signs that the story Scripture is telling is larger than the one many of us inherited.

What Happens When the Lens Is Removed

When the "salvation = heaven" assumption is set aside, the New Testament does not become less clear.

It becomes more coherent.

Suddenly, passages that once seemed to compete begin to align. Saving language appears repeatedly, in many forms, addressing real threats to life. Birth language regains its force. Sonship stops sounding ornamental. Inheritance becomes intelligible again.

Nothing essential is lost.

Much is restored.

The problem was never that Scripture was inconsistent. The problem was that we kept forcing different words to answer the same narrow question.

Letting the Text Name Its Own Categories

One of the most important disciplines in reading Scripture without tradition is refusing to collapse distinct biblical words into a single concept.

The New Testament speaks with more precision than our formulas often allow.

It uses *sozo* for rescue, healing, deliverance, and restoration (Mark 5:34; Luke 8:36; Matthew 14:30). It uses *sōtēria* for the broader salvation-horizon of God's saving work - presently tasted, still being approached, and awaiting future unveiling (Romans 13:11; 1 Peter 1:5, 9; Hebrews 9:28). It uses *gennaō* for birth (John 3:3–5). It uses *huiothesia* for adoption or son-placement (Romans 8:15; Galatians 4:5). It uses *klēronomia* for inheritance (Romans 8:17; 1 Peter 1:4). And it uses *basileia* for Kingdom (Mark 1:15). [4]

When tradition forces these into one thin category called "salvation," precision is lost and confusion follows.

Scripture does not speak that way.

Reading for Function, Not Assumption

Another habit tradition teaches us is to read Scripture mainly for status.

Am I in or out? Saved or not saved? Secure or lost?

Those questions are not meaningless. But the New Testament is often doing more than answering them.

---

[4] Refer to appendix sections for additional insight into the Greek

It is asking about function.

Who is ruling rightly? Who is maturing? Who is being healed? Who is walking as a son? Who is being prepared for inheritance?

When we read functionally, the story begins to move again. The saving act appears not as a badge, but as God's Response to threatened life. Birth appears as capacity. Sonship appears as vocation. Inheritance appears as responsibility.

The story stops sitting still.

Allowing Time to Remain Time

Tradition often compresses Scripture's timeline.

Past, present, and future are collapsed into a single moment. Salvation is spoken of as something that has happened, is happening, and will happen - and then all three are treated as though they must mean exactly the same thing.

The New Testament does not do this.

Paul can say, *"who delivered us... and doth deliver... and will yet deliver us"* (2 Corinthians 1:10). He can also say, *"now is our salvation nearer than when we believed"* (Romans 13:11). Peter can speak of a salvation *"ready to be revealed in the last time,"* while also speaking of believers *"receiving the end of your faith, even the salvation of your souls"* (1 Peter 1:5, 9). Hebrews says Christ will appear the second time *"unto salvation"* (Hebrews 9:28).

Scripture is not confused.

It is simply not forcing every use of saving language to name the same moment.

Reading without tradition means allowing Scripture to keep its temporal distinctions intact.

Learning to Ask Better Questions

Instead of asking, "Is this verse about salvation?"

A more faithful question is: "What is God saving from here?"

Instead of asking, "How does this get someone to heaven?"

We ask, "What kind of life is being restored here? What threat is being confronted? What reality is being named?"

Those questions do not diminish Scripture.

They honor it.

They let the text speak before the system interrupts.

Why This Matters

When Scripture is forced to answer questions it was never primarily asking, readers are left frustrated, divided, or disillusioned.

But when Scripture is allowed to speak on its own terms, it becomes steady again. Demanding. Hopeful. Alive.

We do not need a new Bible.

We need clean eyes.

A Gentler Way Forward

Reading without tradition does not mean rejecting teachers, councils, or history.

It means holding them with humility.

It means allowing Scripture to correct our summaries without feeling threatened. It means searching the Scriptures the way the Bereans did - not with cynicism, but with readiness of mind (Acts 17:11). It means trusting that God's Word is capable of speaking more richly than the formulas we inherited.

This is not about becoming clever.

It is about becoming faithful.

Where This Leads

Once the text is allowed to speak freely, something remarkable happens.

God's saving acts begin to appear everywhere. A single life begins to look less like a one-time transaction and more like a tapestry of rescues, healings, restorations, renewals, births, corrections, and preparations.

Not one thin definition stretched until it tears.

Many saving acts, all held inside God's larger saving purpose.

That is the story we now turn to.

Scripture Index:

- Mark 7:13
- Mark 1:14–15
- John 3:3–5
- Romans 8:14–17
- Mark 5:34
- Luke 8:36
- Matthew 14:30
- Romans 13:11
- 1 Peter 1:5
- 1 Peter 1:9
- Hebrews 9:28
- Romans 8:15
- Galatians 4:5
- Romans 8:17
- 1 Peter 1:4
- 2 Corinthians 1:10
- Acts 17:11

Chapter Seventeen

The Many Saving Acts of a Single Life

If *sozo* is allowed to speak in its biblical register, one quiet realization begins to surface:

A single life may contain many moments of rescue.

This is not a departure from Scripture. It is the pattern Scripture itself reveals. The New Testament does not describe God's saving work as one thin event sealed in the past and never spoken of again. It speaks of God acting to save again and again - whenever life is threatened, diminished, bound, fractured, or breaking.

These are not stages toward a final score.

They are acts of *sozo* - Responses of a faithful God to real conditions in real time.

And those many acts do not create many rival salvations. They belong within the larger horizon Scripture can also call *sōtēria*: the broader saving purpose of God, presently tasted, repeatedly manifested, and ultimately brought to fullness.

Why Scripture Can Speak This Way

Paul says, without embarrassment, that God *"delivered us from so great a death, and doth deliver: in whom we trust that he will yet deliver us"* (2 Corinthians 1:10).

Past. Present. Future.

That language only becomes confusing if every use of salvation language is forced to mean one thin thing every time it appears. But when *sozo* is allowed to name the saving act in context, the language settles. God saves from what threatens life now. He saves again when new threats arise. And He will save when the final enemies of life are confronted.

This does not create many *sōtēriai* in competition with one another. [5]

It reveals many acts of *sozo* within one faithful saving purpose.

Physical Saving Acts

The Gospels are filled with physical acts of *sozo*.

Blind eyes opened. Diseased bodies restored. Crippled bodies strengthened. Death itself interrupted. Jesus tells the woman, "*Thy faith hath made thee whole*" (Mark 5:34). Blind Bartimaeus hears the same saving language: "thy faith hath saved thee" (Luke 18:42). Jairus pleads that his daughter may be healed and live in language that belongs to the same saving world (Mark 5:23). James says plainly, "*the prayer of faith shall save the sick*" (James 5:15).

---

[5] For a clearer explanation of the difference between sozo and soteria refer to appendix G

These moments are not treated as illustrations of some other salvation.

They are acts of *sozo*.

The text does not apologize for this. It does not spiritualize it away. It names the rescue plainly.

When life in the body is threatened, God saves.

Inner Saving Acts

Scripture also recognizes acts of *sozo* within the inner life.

Peace where torment ruled. Soundness where confusion reigned. Release from shame, fear, and inward collapse. The woman in Luke's Gospel does not merely hear that she is excused; she hears, *"Thy faith hath saved thee; go in peace"* (Luke 7:50). The man once possessed is found *"clothed, and in his right mind,"* and the people speak of how he was saved (Luke 8:35–36).

These are not abstract psychological states.

They are real threats to human flourishing.

When God restores peace, clarity, and sanity, He is not doing something less than salvation. He is enacting *sozo* at a level often unseen but deeply felt.

The soul, too, can be rescued.

Spiritual Saving Acts

There are also moments when *sozo* addresses spiritual bondage directly.

Oppression is broken. Demons are expelled. Freedom is restored. In the Gerasene account, the man is not merely calmed; he is liberated. The text says those who saw it "told them by what means he that was possessed of the devils was healed," using the language of being saved (Luke 8:36).

These events are not about spectacle.

They are about relief.

They restore a person's capacity to live, to choose, to relate, and to respond to God.

Spiritual *sozo* is not about power display.

It is about life returned to those who have been bound.

Social Saving Acts

Some of the most overlooked acts of *sozo* in Scripture are social.

The outcast is restored to community. The unclean are brought back near. The excluded are named again as neighbors. The woman with the issue of blood is not only healed; she is publicly restored and called *"Daughter"* (Mark 5:34). The leper who returns in gratitude hears, "thy faith hath made thee whole," in a context where restoration is not merely bodily but social and covenantal (Luke 17:19).

In the ancient world, exclusion was not inconvenience.

It was death by isolation.

When Jesus restores people to community, He is not merely being kind.

He is saving them.

Life requires belonging.

Communal Saving Acts

Scripture also speaks of God saving communities, not just individuals.

Paul speaks of all aboard the ship being preserved from destruction and uses explicit saving language to do it (Acts 27:20, 31, 34). Households are drawn into the life of the gospel together, not merely as private spiritual fragments but as communities being gathered under God's intervention (Acts 16:31–34).

These are not metaphors.

They are acts of preservation, rescue, and realignment among people whose lives are bound up with one another.

God acts to save people together.

And when we step back, we begin to see that such acts are not random. They belong to the wider *sōtēria* horizon of God gathering, preserving, and preparing a people.

Eschatological Salvation

Finally, Scripture speaks not only of many acts of *sozo*, but of the broader salvation-horizon still ahead.

There is a future rescue from corruption, decay, and death itself. Creation waits for deliverance. The sons of God will be revealed. What has been sown in weakness will be raised in strength (Romans 8:19–23; 1 Corinthians 15:42–54). Peter speaks of a salvation *"ready to be revealed in the last time"* (1 Peter 1:5).

Here the language is no longer merely about one immediate act of rescue in a passing crisis.

Here we are standing more clearly in the world of *sōtēria*— the larger outcome toward which all God's saving acts have been moving.

This future salvation does not negate the present acts of *sozo*.

It gathers them.

Each saving act now is a pledge, not a replacement. It is evidence that God saves - and will bring His salvation-purpose to completion.

Why This Does Not Turn Salvation into a Process

Some will worry that speaking of many saving acts turns salvation into something earned or achieved over time.

Scripture does not support that fear.

Sozo is never something we produce. It is always something God does. And the fact that *sozo* may occur again and again does not mean *sōtēria* is a ladder of merit.

It means God is faithful across time.

A Father who intervenes again and again is not negotiating worthiness.

He is responding to need.

2 Corinthians 1:10 does not describe a man climbing upward by effort. It describes a God who keeps intervening because His people keep needing Him.

Repeated acts of *sozo* do not turn *sōtēria* into a process of self-salvation.

They reveal the consistency of God's saving care within a larger saving purpose.

A Life Marked by Rescue

When Scripture is allowed to speak freely, a believer's life does not look like one dramatic rescue followed by maintenance.

It looks like a story punctuated by God's faithfulness.

Moments of danger. Moments of intervention. Moments of restoration.

Again and again.

This is not instability.

It is covenant.

A single life may know many acts of *sozo*.

And all of them belong within the one larger saving horizon of *sōtēria*.

Where This Leads

If *sozo* appears many times across a single life, then *sozo* cannot be the destination.

It must be the means by which God keeps confronting what threatens life along the way.

And if *sōtēria* is the larger horizon that gathers all those saving acts into one purpose, then the question is no longer merely whether God saves.

The question becomes:

What is God saving us for?

That question brings us to the final turn of this section.

Scripture Index:

- 2 Corinthians 1:10
- Mark 5:34
- Luke 18:42
- Mark 5:23
- James 5:15
- Luke 7:50
- Luke 8:35–36
- Luke 17:19
- Acts 27:20
- Acts 27:31
- Acts 27:34
- Acts 16:31–34
- Romans 8:19–23
- 1 Corinthians 15:42–54
- 1 Peter 1:5

Chapter Eighteen

Saved to Become, Not Saved to Escape

Every story has an ending in view.

And the ending we expect quietly shapes how we read everything that comes before it.

For many believers, the story of salvation was told with a single horizon: escape. Salvation was framed as rescue from judgment, from hell, from a doomed world God intended to abandon. Once that rescue was secured, the rest of the Christian life became commentary - important, perhaps, but secondary.

But Scripture tells a different story.

Not a smaller one.

A larger one.

When Escape Became the Goal

At some point in the Church's telling of the gospel, salvation ceased to be heard primarily as God's saving intervention within His creation and became, for many, a ticket out of it.

The gospel was reduced to a question of destination. The language of becoming gave way to the language of arrival. And transformation - once central to the apostolic vision - slowly moved toward the margins (Romans 8:29; 2 Corinthians 3:18).

This was not usually malicious.

It was gradual.

As salvation was compressed into a single moment, the future horizon of God's purpose faded. Sonship became positional rather than functional. Inheritance became abstract. Authority was spiritualized. And the Kingdom became something postponed rather than practiced (Luke 12:32; Romans 8:17).

The story lost its middle.

Why Transformation Quietly Disappeared

When salvation is treated as the end of the story, transformation becomes optional.

Growth becomes admirable but unnecessary. Discipline becomes suspect. Obedience is reframed as legalism. Maturity is encouraged, but rarely expected.

But Scripture never speaks that way.

The New Testament assumes change. It expects formation. It describes lives being shaped, tested, corrected, and prepared—not to earn God's favor, but because God's favor has already been given (Hebrews 12:5–11; Ephesians 4:13–15; Philippians 2:12–13).

God saves, and then He forms.

Not to justify.

But to prepare.

Saved for What?

The New Testament does not shy away from that question.

The saving act rescues from danger, but it also creates capacity. New birth grants access to Kingdom life (John 3:3–5). Sonship confers identity (Romans 8:14–17). Inheritance assigns responsibility (Galatians 4:1–7; 1 Peter 1:4).

God does not rescue people merely to keep them safe.

He rescues them to make them useful.

And this usefulness is not servitude in the degrading sense. It is participation. The sons of God are not ornaments in the Kingdom. They are stewards within it - trained to bear responsibility in alignment with the character of the King (Luke 12:42–44; Matthew 25:21).

Why Salvation Was Never the Destination

If salvation were the destination, Scripture would end with forgiveness.

It does not.

It moves forward to resurrection, inheritance, authority, and glory (Romans 8:17–23; 1 Corinthians 15:42–54; Hebrews 2:10). It speaks of reigning, judging, and restoring (Revelation 5:10; 2 Timothy 2:12; 1 Corinthians 6:2–3). It describes a people prepared to share in God's purposes, not merely enjoy His mercy.

The saving act opens the door.

What lies beyond the door is a life of becoming.

And this is where the broader horizon of *sōtēria* must remain visible. *Sozo* names the rescuing act in context. *Sōtēria* can name the larger saving purpose into which those acts belong. When the two are collapsed, salvation is made smaller than Scripture makes it.

The Fear of Becoming

For many, the idea of becoming is uncomfortable.

It sounds like effort. It sounds like expectation. It sounds like something that could be measured - or failed.

But Scripture does not present becoming as anxious striving. It presents it as growth under care.

A child does not earn maturity. They grow into it.

So do the sons of God.

Paul says believers are being transformed *"from glory to glory"* by the Spirit of the Lord (2 Corinthians 3:18). Hebrews speaks of sons disciplined by a Father who loves them (Hebrews 12:6–10). Growth is not the denial of grace.

It is one of grace's intended effects.

The Call Back to Sonship

Jesus did not gather disciples merely to secure their escape.

He gathered them to teach them how to live under God's reign.

He corrected them. He trained them. He entrusted them with authority gradually. He spoke of thrones, not just forgiveness (Luke 22:29–30). He promised inheritance, not merely safety

(Luke 12:32). He spoke of fruitfulness, stewardship, and readiness (John 15:8, 16; Matthew 24:45–47).

This was not a departure from grace.

It was grace's intention.

God's favor does not end with rescue.

It moves toward restoration.

Inheritance Changes the Story

When inheritance returns to the center of the gospel, everything shifts.

Suffering gains meaning. Discipline gains purpose. Obedience gains direction.

The Christian life is no longer about waiting to leave the world behind. It becomes preparation to participate in what God is doing within it - and beyond it (Romans 8:17–19; Hebrews 12:11).

Inheritance does not make the gospel harsher.

It makes it larger.

A Larger Ending

The story Scripture tells does not end with believers escaping earth.

It ends with sons revealed, creation restored, and the Kingdom fully expressed (Romans 8:19–23; Revelation 21:1–5; 22:1–5).

Salvation is woven throughout that story - not as its conclusion, but as its faithful companion along the way.

God saves again and again.

And each act of *sozo* moves His people within the larger horizon of *sōtēria*, closer to what they were always meant to become.

Where This Leaves Us

Salvation was never meant to terminate in relief alone. The saving acts of God are holy, necessary, and full of mercy, but Scripture never presents those acts as the whole horizon. Sozo names the ways God intervenes when life is threatened - when He rescues, restores, heals, delivers, and preserves. But the New Testament does not stop at those saving acts. It keeps opening outward toward the larger salvation-horizon into which those acts belong.

And beneath that whole movement is the agape love of God. Not a thin sentiment. Not mere pity. Not a passing tenderness that pulls back at the edge of ruin and goes no further. Agape moves toward restoration. Agape reaches into what is broken and refuses to leave it there. Agape does not merely interrupt destruction; it labors toward wholeness, toward maturity, toward sonship, toward the inheritance prepared under the reign of the Son.

This is why the gospel cannot end in escape. It cannot climax in survival alone. It cannot be reduced to a message of departure. The saving acts of God are glorious, but they are not the final word. They clear what would have swallowed us. They confront what would have deformed us. They break what would have held us. But the broader purpose of God moves beyond rescue alone. It moves toward becoming. Toward sons brought to glory. Toward inheritance unveiled. Toward creation itself answering the reign of God.

So let the smaller gospel fall away. Let the frightened gospel fall away. Let the gospel that ends in escape give way to the gospel of the Kingdom. For we were not saved merely from. We were saved toward. Toward likeness. Toward maturity. Toward inheritance. Toward the full outworking of what the love of God intended all along.

This is the larger mercy.

This is the deeper gospel.

Not saved to escape.

Saved to become.

And when the purpose of God stands complete, it will not merely be seen that He performed saving acts on behalf of His people. It will be seen that every rescue, every restoration, every deliverance, and every healing was carried forward by agape into something greater - that He was bringing many sons to glory, preparing a people fit for His Kingdom, and unveiling a salvation far larger than escape.

Scripture Index:

- Romans 8:29
- 2 Corinthians 3:18
- Luke 12:32
- Romans 8:17
- Hebrews 12:5–11
- Ephesians 4:13–15
- Philippians 2:12–13
- John 3:3–5
- Romans 8:14–17
- Galatians 4:1–7
- 1 Peter 1:4
- Luke 12:42–44
- Matthew 25:21
- Romans 8:17–23
- 1 Corinthians 15:42–54
- Hebrews 2:10
- Revelation 5:10
- 2 Timothy 2:12
- 1 Corinthians 6:2–3
- Luke 22:29–30
- John 15:8
- John 15:16
- Matthew 24:45–47
- Hebrews 12:11
- Revelation 21:1–5
- Revelation 22:1–5

Appendix A

The Use of σῴζω (Sozo) in the New Testament

A Textual and Contextual Categorization

(Textual, Not Traditional)

Purpose and Scope

This appendix documents the use of the Greek verb **σῴζω** (*sozo*) and its immediate cognates in the New Testament. Its purpose is not to construct a systematic doctrine of salvation, but to observe and categorize how the New Testament authors themselves use the term across a range of literary and situational contexts.

Only passages in which *sozo* or a direct verbal or nominal cognate appears in the Greek text are included. Each occurrence is categorized according to immediate literary context, narrative function, and semantic force, without importing later theological systems or assumptions.

Meaning is derived from usage, not from post-biblical doctrinal synthesis.

Sozo in First-Century Greek Usage

The New Testament's use of **σῴζω** (*sozo*) does not represent a novel or exclusively religious redefinition of the term. The word appears throughout the Greek-speaking world of the first century as a common verb of rescue, recovery, preservation, and restoration.

In non-biblical Greek literature, *sozo* is regularly used to describe:

- recovery from illness
- deliverance from physical danger
- preservation through crisis
- survival in war or disaster
- restoration of well-being, stability, or wholeness

The term carries no inherent reference to the afterlife, eternal destiny, or post-mortem judgment. Its semantic range is situational, not metaphysical. Meaning is determined by the condition from which one is being saved, not by a fixed theological category.[1]

This usage is well documented in classical and Hellenistic sources, including medical writings, historical narratives, and ordinary correspondence, where *sozo* functions as a practical verb describing tangible outcomes rather than abstract states.[2]

Second Temple Jewish literature written in Greek, especially the Septuagint, reflects this same pattern. *Sozo* is used to translate Hebrew terms related to deliverance, healing, rescue, and preservation, frequently in contexts involving physical danger, national survival, covenantal preservation, or restoration from affliction.[3]

Against this linguistic background, the New Testament's use of *sozo* appears continuous rather than innovative. Jesus and the apostles use the word in ways consistent with its established meaning, applying it to bodily healing, rescue from danger, deliverance from oppression, and restoration from the effects of sin. Even where *sozo* appears in future-oriented or eschatological contexts, the word itself does not change meaning. What changes is the object of deliverance.

This continuity strongly suggests that later reductions of *sozo* to a singular concept of "eternal salvation" represent a post-biblical doctrinal narrowing rather than first-century lexical usage.

References for This Section

1. BDAG, s.v. "σῴζω."

2. Louw & Nida, *Greek-English Lexicon of the New Testament Based on Semantic Domains*, Domains 21.21–21.29.

3. Septuagint usage, especially Exodus, Psalms, and Isaiah (LXX).

4. Joel B. Green, *Body, Soul, and Human Life*.

5. N. T. Wright, *Jesus and the Victory of God*.

Methodological Commitments

This appendix operates under the following controls:

1. No verse is included unless *sozo* or a direct cognate is present in the Greek text.
2. Categories are determined by immediate context, not by later theological expectations.
3. No passage is assumed to refer to eternal destiny unless the text itself clearly indicates a future eschatological horizon.
4. Judicial or forensic interpretations are noted only where the text itself employs legal or courtroom imagery.
5. Descriptive clarity is prioritized over doctrinal harmonization.

A Note on the Term "Forensic"

In this appendix, the word **forensic** is used in its theological sense, not in its modern association with scientific investigation or criminal analysis.

The term derives from the Latin *forum*, referring to a public court or judicial setting. In theological discourse, a forensic framework understands salvation primarily as a legal declaration: a verdict in which a person is pronounced innocent, acquitted, or righteous, without reference to internal transformation or restoration.[1]

Within a forensic model:

- sin is treated primarily as a legal offense

- salvation is framed primarily as a judicial verdict

- God is portrayed primarily as judge

- righteousness is understood as declared rather than enacted

This legal framing became increasingly dominant in Western theology, especially after Augustine and later in the Protestant Reformation, where justification was often articulated chiefly in juridical terms.[2]

When this appendix describes a passage as non-forensic, it does not deny forgiveness, mercy, or justification. It indicates that the text itself is not operating primarily with courtroom imagery. In such passages, sin is presented as a condition, bondage, corruption, or state of loss, and *sozo* functions as rescue, healing, restoration, or preservation rather than as legal pronouncement.

This distinction allows the New Testament texts to retain their own categories rather than being retrofitted into later theological models.

Category I - Physical Healing

In these passages, *sozo* clearly denotes bodily healing or restoration from physical affliction.

- Matthew 9:21–22
- Mark 5:23
- Mark 5:34

- Mark 6:56

- Mark 10:52

- Luke 8:48

- Luke 17:19

- Luke 18:42

- James 5:15

Contextual Observation: In each case, *sozo* functions medically or bodily rather than judicially. Translating the term as "heal" or "make whole" often aligns more closely with narrative intent than importing later doctrinal assumptions about eternal destiny.[3]

Category II - Rescue from Immediate Danger

In these passages, *sozo* refers to rescue from physical peril, destruction, or immediate loss of life.

- Matthew 8:25

- Matthew 14:30

- Acts 27:20, 31, 34

- Hebrews 11:7

- Jude 5

Contextual Observation: These uses are entirely non-forensic and demonstrate *sozo* as a common Greek verb for preservation from danger, disaster, or death.[4]

Category III - Deliverance from Demonic Oppression

In these passages, *sozo* denotes restoration from demonic domination or oppressive spiritual bondage.

- Luke 8:36

Contextual Observation: The restoration includes more than the expulsion of spirits. The person is returned to mental clarity, relational dignity, and social intelligibility. The emphasis is restorative and integrative.

Category IV - Restoration from Sin or Its Effects (Non-Forensic)

In these passages, *sozo* is connected explicitly to sin, but not primarily through courtroom imagery.

- Matthew 1:21
- Luke 7:50
- Luke 19:10

Contextual Observation: Sin is treated as a destructive condition requiring rescue and restoration, not merely as a legal charge requiring acquittal.[5]

Category V - Communal or Covenantal Preservation

In these passages, *sozo* refers to the preservation or deliverance of a people, not merely an isolated individual.

- Acts 2:47
- Acts 15:11

- Romans 11:26

Contextual Observation: These passages emphasize covenantal continuity, communal identity, and the saving activity of God among a people. The focus is not limited to private conversion experience.

Category VI - Present Participation in Salvation

These passages use *sozo* language in the present tense or with present participatory force, indicating lived participation in God's saving activity.

- 1 Corinthians 1:18
- 2 Corinthians 2:15
- Philippians 2:12
- Hebrews 7:25

Contextual Observation: The language describes present experience of divine saving action, not progressive self-salvation or merit accumulation. The emphasis is participation, not acquisition.[6]

Category VII - Future or Eschatological Deliverance

In these passages, *sozo* refers to future rescue, vindication, or deliverance in relation to the coming judgment or consummation.

- Matthew 10:22
- Matthew 24:13

- Romans 5:9–10

- Romans 10:9–13

- 1 Thessalonians 5:9

- Hebrews 9:28

- 1 Peter 1:5

Contextual Observation: These passages are future-oriented, but the text does not require "hell" to be the sole or automatic object of salvation. The emphasis remains deliverance in the face of coming judgment, wrath, or final corruption.[7]

Category VIII - General or Summary Uses

These passages use *sozo* in a broader or less tightly specified sense, where the exact object of rescue is not narrowly defined by the verse itself.

- Acts 4:12

- Acts 16:30–31

Contextual Observation: In such cases, meaning must be supplied by larger narrative and theological context. The term itself remains open enough to require contextual restraint.

Key Textual Observations

1. *Sozo* does not inherently mean "saved from hell."

2. The term is applied to bodies, minds, communities, nations, and futures.

3. Each occurrence refers to a divine saving act rather than a humanly produced process.

4. The New Testament does not present *sozo* as a single universal conversion event.

5. Meaning is always determined by context, not by inherited doctrinal shorthand.

Function of This Appendix

This appendix serves as a lexical and contextual control document for the book. Interpretive claims regarding *sozo* should be tested against these categories rather than against later traditional reductions.

This appendix does not attempt to settle every theological dispute.

It exists to preserve textual clarity.

References

1. BDAG, *A Greek-English Lexicon of the New Testament and Other Early Christian Literature*, 3rd ed., s.v. "σῴζω."

2. Alister E. McGrath, *Iustitia Dei: A History of the Christian Doctrine of Justification*, 3rd ed. (Cambridge: Cambridge University Press, 2005).

3. Joel B. Green, *Body, Soul, and Human Life* (Grand Rapids: Baker Academic, 2008).

4. Louw and Nida, *Greek-English Lexicon of the New Testament Based on Semantic Domains*, 2nd ed.

5. N. T. Wright, *Jesus and the Victory of God* (Minneapolis: Fortress Press, 1996).

6. John M. G. Barclay, *Paul and the Gift* (Grand Rapids: Eerdmans, 2015).

7. George Eldon Ladd, *The Presence of the Future* (Grand Rapids: Eerdmans, 1974).

Appendix B

Distinguishing Salvation (Sozo), New Birth, and Sonship

A Textual and Structural Clarification

Purpose and Scope

This appendix exists to distinguish three concepts that are frequently conflated in modern Christian language but are treated distinctly in the New Testament:

1. Salvation (σῴζω / *sozo*)
2. New Birth (γεννάω ἄνωθεν, γεννηθῇ ἐξ ὕδατος καὶ πνεύματος)
3. Sonship (υἱοθεσία; τέκνα Θεοῦ)

Contemporary theology often compresses these realities into a single conversion moment. The New Testament does not. Each term serves a different function, occupies a different place in the biblical narrative, and addresses a different aspect of God's work in humanity.

This appendix does not attempt to harmonize these concepts into one doctrinal formula. It documents their distinct functions as they appear in Scripture.

I. Salvation (*Sozo*)

Definition and Function

In the New Testament, *sozo* denotes a concrete act of divine intervention by which a person, group, or situation is rescued, healed, restored, preserved, or delivered from a defined threat, condition, or state of loss.[1]

As shown throughout this work, *sozo* is applied to:

- physical healing
- rescue from danger
- deliverance from demonic oppression
- restoration from the effects of sin
- covenantal preservation
- future eschatological deliverance

Each use is context-dependent and event-oriented.

Key Observations

- *Sozo* is received, not achieved.
- It addresses conditions, not identity.
- It may occur more than once within a single life.
- It does not, by itself, establish sonship, inheritance, or maturity.

The New Testament does not present *sozo* as a single, universal conversion event that permanently exhausts God's saving activity in a person's life.

II. New Birth

Definition and Function

New birth refers to the generation of new life by the Spirit, enabling a person to perceive and participate in the Kingdom of God. Jesus introduces this concept in John 3 using the language of birth rather than the language of legal acquittal.[2]

The imagery is ontological, not merely forensic. New birth describes the coming into existence of a new kind of life, not merely the resolution of a legal charge.

Key Observations

- New birth is an act, not a gradual process.
- It produces capacity, not maturity.
- It enables one to see and enter the Kingdom (John 3:3, 5).
- It is not equated with *sozo* in Scripture.

A person may experience acts of salvation without new birth, just as one newly born must still grow, mature, and be formed.

A Linguistic Note on "Born Again" / "From Above"

The Greek phrase commonly translated "born again" in John 3 (γεννηθῇ ἄνωθεν) carries a semantic range that includes both repetition ("again") and origin ("from above"). The latter sense emphasizes not merely the event of birth, but the source of life itself.[1]

The verb *γεννάω*, often rendered "born," also carries the sense of begetting or fathering, placing emphasis on divine origin rather than human initiative. This suggests that new birth is not merely a change of status, but the impartation of life sourced from God Himself.

John 3 does not explicitly develop the full doctrine of sonship, but the language of divine begetting naturally gestures in that direction. New birth establishes origin and capacity. Sonship later names identity, relationship, and inheritance. The two realities are related, but the New Testament does not treat them as interchangeable.

This appendix preserves the connection without collapsing the categories.

III. Sonship

Definition and Function

Sonship refers to relational identity and inheritance status within God's household. It is expressed in Scripture through:

- adoption (*υἱοθεσία*)
- being led by the Spirit
- conformity to the image of Christ
- participation in inheritance and authority [3]

Sonship is identity-defining, not merely experiential.

Key Observations

- Sonship is grounded in relationship, not rescue.

- It carries inheritance, not merely forgiveness.

- It involves both status and formation.

- It is presented as the intended outcome of God's redemptive work (Hebrews 2:10).

Scripture consistently frames God's purpose not merely as producing forgiven individuals, but as bringing many sons to glory.

IV. Structural Relationship Between the Three

The New Testament presents salvation, new birth, and sonship as related but non-identical realities.

- *Sozo* describes what God does for a person.

- New birth describes what God generates in a person.

- Sonship describes who that person becomes in relation to the Father and His household.

When these categories are conflated:

- salvation is mistaken for identity

- identity is reduced to an event

- maturity becomes optional

- inheritance becomes symbolic

These reductions do not arise from the biblical text itself. They arise from imprecise language imposed upon it.

V. A Note on the Scriptural Pattern Leading to New Birth

Scripture does not present new birth as a mechanical formula. It does, however, reveal a recognizable relational pattern by which God awakens, draws, and brings people into participation in His Kingdom.

That pattern appears across the Gospels and Acts and may be summarized as follows:

God draws the person toward Himself, awakening desire and attention (John 6:44). The Word is received as seed, planted in the heart and mind (Mark 4:14; James 1:18). The Spirit of truth brings conviction - not condemnation - exposing reality and producing awareness (John 16:8; Romans 8:1). This awakening gives rise to godly sorrow, leading toward repentance rather than shame (Second Corinthians 7:10). Repentance marks a turning of mind and direction, preparing the person for transformation (Acts 2:38). New birth occurs through being born of water and Spirit, granting the capacity to see and enter the Kingdom of God (John 3:3, 5), without implying maturity, inheritance, or completion. Baptism functions in Scripture as a participatory act of cleansing, burial, and transition - an embodied Response through which God applies what He has already accomplished, rather than a performative display for observers (Acts 22:16; Romans 6:3–4). The infilling of the Holy Spirit follows as empowerment and life, often accompanied by outward manifestation (Acts 2:4; Acts 10:44–48).

This pattern describes how God brings a person into new life. It does not describe how a person earns salvation. Acts of *sozo* may occur at multiple points along this pattern, but new birth itself marks the beginning of Kingdom participation, not the completion of God's work.

VI. Function of This Appendix

Appendix B serves as a terminological and structural control for this book. Any claim regarding salvation, belief, baptism, new birth, sonship, inheritance, or Kingdom participation should be evaluated in light of these distinctions.

This appendix does not advance a separate system.

It preserves biblical clarity.

References

1. BDAG, *A Greek-English Lexicon of the New Testament and Other Early Christian Literature*, 3rd ed., s.v. "σῴζω."

2. Joel B. Green, *Body, Soul, and Human Life* (Grand Rapids: Baker Academic, 2008).

3. James D. G. Dunn, *The Theology of Paul the Apostle* (Grand Rapids: Eerdmans, 1998).

4. N. T. Wright, *Paul and the Faithfulness of God* (Minneapolis: Fortress Press, 2013).

5. George Eldon Ladd, *The Presence of the Future* (Grand Rapids: Eerdmans, 1974).

6. Alister E. McGrath, *Iustitia Dei: A History of the Christian Doctrine of Justification*, 3rd ed. (Cambridge: Cambridge University Press, 2005).

Appendix C

The Kingdom of God and the Kingdom of Heaven

Language, Context, and First-Century Understanding

Purpose and Scope

This appendix clarifies the New Testament language of the **Kingdom of God** and the **Kingdom of Heaven**, especially as these phrases would have been heard by first-century Jewish audiences in the context of Jesus' proclamation.

Modern Christian teaching often reduces "the Kingdom" to:

- a synonym for heaven after death, or
- a future destination entered at conversion

The New Testament does not support these reductions. This appendix documents:

- how Kingdom language functions in Scripture
- how it aligns with Jewish expectation
- how it differs from later theological assumptions

Terminological Clarification

Kingdom of God vs. Kingdom of Heaven

The phrases **Kingdom of God** (*βασιλεία τοῦ Θεοῦ*) and **Kingdom of Heaven** (*βασιλεία τῶν οὐρανῶν*) do not refer to two different kingdoms.

- **Kingdom of God** appears predominantly in Mark, Luke, John, and Paul.

- **Kingdom of Heaven** appears almost exclusively in Matthew.

This difference reflects Jewish reverential speech rather than theological distinction. Matthew, writing with a stronger Jewish orientation, frequently uses "heaven" as a circumlocution for God, consistent with Second Temple Jewish practice.[1]

Both phrases refer to the same Kingdom reality.

What "Kingdom" Meant in the First Century

In first-century Jewish thought, **kingdom** did not primarily mean:

- a location
- a realm in the sky
- a post-mortem destination

Rather, βασιλεία regularly denotes:

- reign
- rule

- authority
- active governance

The **Kingdom of God** therefore refers first to God's rule being exercised, not to people going somewhere else.[2]

To announce that the Kingdom was "at hand" was to declare that God's authority was drawing near, pressing into present reality, and demanding Response.

The Kingdom in the Teaching of Jesus

Jesus' central proclamation is the Kingdom.

He does not move through Galilee primarily announcing heaven as destination, nor does He summarize His message as a method for individual escape. He announces the nearness of God's reign:

- *"Repent: for the kingdom of heaven is at hand"* (Matthew 4:17)
- *"If I cast out devils by the Spirit of God, then the kingdom of God is come unto you"* (Matthew 12:28)
- *"The kingdom of God is in the midst of you"* or *"among you"* (Luke 17:21)

These statements are active and present-oriented, even where the Kingdom also retains a future dimension.

Jesus also speaks of the Kingdom as something that can be:

- seen (John 3:3)

- entered (John 3:5)

- received (Mark 10:15)

- sought first (Matthew 6:33)

- inherited (Matthew 25:34)

None of these verbs require death as the primary point of access.

Kingdom and New Birth

Jesus' conversation with Nicodemus establishes a crucial boundary.

New birth is not identical with inheritance, maturity, or completed Kingdom participation. It is the generation of life from above that enables perception and entry:

- *"Except a man be born again, he cannot see the kingdom of God"* (John 3:3)

- *"Except a man be born of water and of the Spirit, he cannot enter into the kingdom of God"* (John 3:5)

New birth addresses origin and capacity, not the full outworking of authority, maturity, or inheritance.

The Kingdom is not entered by mere legal status, but by life sourced from God.[3]

Kingdom and Sonship

If new birth enables entry, sonship frames mature participation.

Jesus repeatedly speaks in familial language:

- sons of the Kingdom
- children of the Father
- heirs
- stewards

This language is not ornamental. It is structural.

Inheritance presupposes:

- relationship
- formation
- maturity

The New Testament does not present the Kingdom merely as a gift to be noticed or a realm to be visited. It presents the Kingdom as the sphere of God's reign in which sons are formed, trained, and ultimately prepared to share in Christ's rule (Romans 8:17; Revelation 5:10).

For that reason, sonship must not be reduced to status alone. In the New Testament, sonship is both relational and formative.

The Kingdom Is Present, Growing, and Future

Jesus describes the Kingdom in ways that are present, developmental, and future without contradiction.

The Kingdom is:

- present in Christ's ministry
- growing through the work of God

- future in its fullness and consummation

Jesus compares the Kingdom to seed, leaven, growth, and harvest (Mark 4:26–32; Matthew 13:33). These images do not suggest confusion. They suggest inauguration, development, and completion.

The Kingdom is therefore best understood as:

- inaugurated in Christ

- advancing through His reign and people

- consummated at the end of the age

Acts of *sozo* participate in this Kingdom movement, but *sozo* does not define the Kingdom. The Kingdom is the larger reign-context in which God's saving acts occur.

Common Modern Misreadings

When Kingdom language is collapsed into "going to heaven," several distortions follow:

- salvation is treated as the goal rather than as one of the means by which God confronts what threatens life

- discipleship is reduced or postponed

- inheritance is abstracted

- authority is deferred without formation

- sonship is reduced to status rather than maturity

These reductions do not reflect the Kingdom Jesus proclaimed.

Function of This Appendix

Appendix C serves as a conceptual control for Kingdom language throughout this book.

It helps preserve four distinctions:

- the Kingdom is not equated with the afterlife
- salvation is not mistaken for inheritance
- new birth is not treated as completion
- sonship is understood as participatory, formative, and inheritance-oriented

The Kingdom is the larger context in which God's saving work operates.

It is not the reward that salvation merely secures after death.

References

1. BDAG, s.v. "βασιλεία."

2. N. T. Wright, *Jesus and the Victory of God* (Minneapolis: Fortress Press, 1996).

3. George Eldon Ladd, *The Presence of the Future* (Grand Rapids: Eerdmans, 1974).

4. Joachim Jeremias, *The Parables of Jesus* (London: SCM Press, 1972).

5. Second Temple Jewish literature (Psalms of Solomon; Dead Sea Scrolls).

Scripture Index:

- Matthew 4:17
- Matthew 12:28
- Luke 17:21
- John 3:3
- John 3:5
- Mark 10:15
- Matthew 6:33
- Matthew 25:34
- Romans 8:17
- Revelation 5:10
- Mark 4:26–32
- Matthew 13:33

Appendix D

How the Early Church Lost the Gospel of the Kingdom

From Reign to Destination, From Participation to Belief

Purpose and Scope

This appendix examines how the **Gospel of the Kingdom**, as proclaimed by Jesus and continued by the apostles, gradually lost its central place in Christian emphasis and was increasingly reframed as a gospel focused primarily on individual salvation and the afterlife.

The purpose here is not to assign blame, condemn historical figures, or suggest wholesale apostasy. It is to trace a long, cumulative shift in emphasis - a shift that unfolded across centuries as the Church moved through new languages, cultures, political realities, and philosophical frameworks.

The gospel was not erased.

It was reframed.

The Gospel Jesus Preached

Jesus' central proclamation was clear and consistent:

- *"Repent: for the kingdom of heaven is at hand"* (Matthew 4:17)

- *"The time is fulfilled, and the kingdom of God is at hand"* (Mark 1:14–15)

- *"I must preach the kingdom of God to other cities also: for therefore am I sent"* (Luke 4:43)

This announcement was not a synonym for heaven after death, nor merely another way of saying private salvation. In first-century Jewish thought, kingdom referred primarily to reign, rule, and authority. Jesus declared that God's rule was drawing near and breaking into the present through His words, works, and person.

Within this proclamation, acts of *sozo* functioned as signs and enactments of the Kingdom:

- the sick were healed

- the oppressed were delivered

- sins were forgiven

- the outcast were restored

These acts did not replace the Kingdom message.

They revealed it.

The Apostolic Continuation

The book of Acts preserves this Kingdom-centered framework.

- Jesus teaches the apostles *"the things pertaining to the kingdom of God"* after His resurrection (Acts 1:3).

- Philip preaches *"the things concerning the kingdom of God, and the name of Jesus Christ"* (Acts 8:12).

- Paul speaks *"of the kingdom of God"* throughout his ministry (Acts 19:8; 20:25; 28:23, 31).

Salvation language appears frequently in apostolic preaching and writing, but it appears within the larger Kingdom story rather than as its substitute.

The First Major Shift: Language and Audience

As the gospel moved from a primarily Jewish setting into the broader Greco-Roman world, the Church faced a linguistic and conceptual transition.

Jewish hearers already understood Kingdom language through Scripture, covenant, temple, exile, restoration, and the hope of God's reign over His people and the nations. Gentile hearers often approached reality through different categories, including:

- the immortality of the soul
- the relative inferiority of the material world
- salvation conceived as escape from bodily or earthly existence

This shift did not happen instantly or uniformly. But over time, Kingdom language was increasingly translated into categories more familiar to Hellenistic thought, and emphasis began to move from God's reign in history toward the soul's destiny beyond it.

The Second Major Shift: From Embodied Participation to Abstract Belief

In the New Testament, allegiance to Jesus involved:

- repentance
- baptism
- obedience
- community formation
- Spirit-formed life under a new Lord

Belief was not mere agreement. It was allegiance, trust, and reorientation under the reign of Christ.

As catechetical instruction developed and doctrinal controversies intensified, the faith increasingly came to be defined by assent to formal statements, especially concerning Christ's nature and work. These clarifications were often necessary and valuable. But over time, belief could be heard more as intellectual agreement than as participatory obedience.

The gospel became easier to describe as something to affirm than as a reign to enter.

The Third Major Shift: Institutionalization and Empire

With the legalization and later imperial favor of Christianity in the fourth century, the Church underwent a major social transformation.

- Christianity moved from marginal movement to protected and eventually dominant religion.

- Kingdom language, once subversive, became more difficult to preach in the same way inside an imperial framework.

- Emphasis shifted toward institutional stability, orthodoxy, social order, and sacramental administration.

The Kingdom was not denied, but it was increasingly relocated - either into the distant future or into a largely spiritualized realm - while its disruptive, present-tense force was muted.

The Fourth Major Shift: Judicial Framing of Salvation

As Western theology developed, especially through Augustine and later in medieval and Reformation thought, salvation was increasingly framed in juridical terms:

- sin as guilt
- righteousness as legal standing
- salvation as acquittal or justification

These categories are not foreign to Scripture. The problem is not their presence, but their dominance. When judicial categories became primary, other biblical frames - Kingdom, participation, restoration, inheritance, sonship, and embodied transformation - were increasingly subordinated.

Salvation was narrowed to verdict.

The gospel became, for many, more a solution to guilt than an announcement of reign.

The Resulting Gospel

By the modern period, the gospel was often summarized in terms such as:

- how individuals are forgiven
- how they avoid judgment
- how they secure heaven after death

None of these concerns are illegitimate.

But they are partial.

When they become central, the larger biblical story recedes. The Kingdom becomes background. Sonship becomes symbolic. Inheritance is postponed. Discipleship becomes optional or secondary.

What Was Lost - and What Was Not

It is important to state clearly what this appendix does **not** claim:

- The Church did not lose Christ.
- The Church did not lose Scripture.
- The Church did not lose every truth about salvation.

What was gradually lost was emphasis, proportion, and imagination.

The Gospel of the Kingdom did not disappear.

It was crowded out.

Why This Matters for This Book

This historical shift helps explain why, in modern Christian language:

- salvation is often treated as the goal rather than as one of the means by which God confronts what threatens life and brings people into contact with the reality of His Kingdom
- baptism is reduced to symbol
- sonship is underdeveloped
- inheritance is postponed or abstracted
- the Kingdom feels distant rather than near

Recovering the Gospel of the Kingdom does not require rejecting the faith we inherited.

It requires placing salvation back into the story it was always meant to serve.

Function of This Appendix

Appendix D provides a historical lens for reading the arguments of this book.

It explains why the questions raised in these chapters often feel unfamiliar, and why recovering biblical language can feel less like novelty and more like rediscovery.

References

- N. T. Wright, *Jesus and the Victory of God*
- George Eldon Ladd, *The Presence of the Future*
- Alister E. McGrath, *Iustitia Dei*
- Jaroslav Pelikan, *The Christian Tradition*, Vols. 1–2
- Everett Ferguson, *Baptism in the Early Church*
- Joachim Jeremias, *The Parables of Jesus*

Scripture Index:

- Matthew 4:17
- Mark 1:14–15
- Luke 4:43
- Acts 1:3
- Acts 8:12
- Acts 19:8
- Acts 20:25
- Acts 28:23
- Acts 28:31

Appendix E

Key Gospel Words Reexamined

A Lexical and Theological Control Appendix

Purpose and Scope

This appendix addresses a recurring problem encountered throughout this book: the quiet reshaping of biblical words by later theological tradition.

Over time, certain Greek terms central to the gospel message have been:

- narrowed in meaning
- redefined by doctrinal systems
- abstracted away from their original relational, covenantal, and experiential force

When these words are misunderstood, the gospel itself is subtly altered—not by rejecting Scripture, but by speaking Scripture with foreign definitions.

This appendix does not seek to dismantle faith.

It seeks to restore vocabulary.

Its purpose is lexical, grammatical, and theological. Each entry identifies a key Greek term, notes its semantic range, summarizes its function in the New Testament, identifies common traditional drift, and provides a corrective aligned with the textual framework of this book.

How to Read This Appendix

These entries are not exhaustive lexicon articles. They are controlled lexical summaries designed to stabilize how key words are used throughout this work.

They are intended to function as:

- a lexical checkpoint
- a theological guardrail
- a reference tool for maintaining consistency

Readers should approach these sections not as arguments to win, but as lenses for clearer reading.

E.1 - Χάρις (*Charis*)

Favor That Gives, Not Power That Forces

Lexical Range: favor, goodwill, gracious disposition, gift freely given, benefaction.[1]

Textual Function: *Charis* describes God's favorable initiative toward humanity. It is relational, not mechanical; generous, not coercive. It precedes human Response and creates the context in which Response becomes possible.

Common Drift: Grace is often treated as an impersonal substance, force, or power that automatically produces obedience or transformation.

Corrective: Grace gives access, favor, generosity, and relational opening. It does not bypass trust, obedience, formation, or maturity. Grace makes these possible. It does not replace them.

E.2 - Ἔλεος (*Eleos*)

Mercy That Withholds Judgment

Lexical Range: mercy, compassion, pity shown to the guilty, needy, or afflicted.

Textual Function: *Eleos* addresses guilt, misery, and exposure to deserved judgment. It operates in both relational and judicial contexts.

Common Drift: Mercy is often merged indistinguishably with grace.

Corrective: Mercy and grace are related, but not identical. Mercy withholds deserved judgment. Grace extends undeserved favor. Mercy addresses condemnation; grace establishes access and relationship.

E.3 - Πίστις (*Pistis*)

Trust, Allegiance, and Faithfulness

Lexical Range: trust, confidence, loyalty, faithfulness, allegiance.

Textual Function: In first-century usage, *pistis* often includes relational loyalty and covenantal trust, not merely internal agreement. It can describe both trusting Response and ongoing fidelity.

Common Drift: Faith is often reduced to agreement with propositions about God or Christ.

Corrective: Biblical faith is not mere mental assent. It is trust directed toward a person, allegiance rendered to a king, and fidelity expressed in life.

E.4 - Πιστεύω (*Pisteuō*)

To Entrust, Commit, and Rely Upon

Lexical Range: to trust, to entrust oneself, to rely upon, to commit oneself to.

Textual Function: *Pisteuō* describes relational action, not abstract opinion. It is directional and participatory.

Common Drift: Belief is often treated as intellectual agreement alone.

Corrective: To believe in Scripture is not merely to think something is true. It is to entrust oneself to the One proclaimed, to respond in trust, and to align life with that confession.

E.5 - Μετάνοια (*Metanoia*)

Reorientation, Not Regret

Lexical Range: change of mind, reorientation, alteration of perception, redirection.

Textual Function: *Metanoia* describes turning in Response to the nearness of God's reign. It is not merely sorrow, though sorrow may precede it.

Common Drift: Repentance is often collapsed into emotional remorse, guilt, or regret.

Corrective: Repentance is not merely feeling bad. It is a turning of mind, allegiance, and direction in Response to truth.

E.6 - Σῴζω (*Sozo*)

Rescue, Healing, Preservation, Restoration

Lexical Range: to save, rescue, heal, preserve, deliver, restore.[2]

Textual Function: *Sozo* denotes concrete acts of divine intervention addressing specific threats, conditions, or states of loss. Its meaning is governed by context.

Common Drift: *Sozo* is routinely collapsed into "saved from hell."

Corrective: *Sozo* is a broad rescue word. It may refer to bodily healing, rescue from danger, deliverance from oppression, restoration from sin's effects, covenant preservation, or future deliverance. It names saving acts, not one fixed doctrinal formula. Full treatment appears in Appendix A.

E.7 - Σωτηρία (*Sōtēria*)

The Broader Salvation Horizon

Lexical Range: salvation, deliverance, preservation, safety, rescue, welfare.

Textual Function: *Sōtēria* often denotes the broader salvation-horizon, outcome, or sphere resulting from God's saving work. It can carry present, future, and corporate dimensions.

Common Drift: *Sōtēria* is often treated as synonymous with heaven after death, or flattened into the same narrow meaning as *sozo*.

Corrective: *Sōtēria* should not be collapsed into mere destination language. It often names the larger reality within which repeated acts of *sozo* occur and toward which God's saving purpose moves.

E.8 - Βασιλεία (*Basileia*)

Reign, Not Merely Realm

Lexical Range: kingship, reign, rule, dominion, authority.

Textual Function: *Basileia* refers primarily to active rule or exercised authority, not simply a location.

Common Drift: The Kingdom is often equated with heaven after death or with a distant realm.

Corrective: The Kingdom is God's reign exercised in reality. It is the larger context in which God's saving acts occur. Full treatment appears in Appendix C.

E.9 - Γεννάω ἄνωθεν (*Gennāō Anōthen*)

Born or Fathered from Above

Lexical Range: to be born, begotten, generated, fathered from above.

Textual Function: This language emphasizes divine origin. It describes the generation of life sourced from above.

Common Drift: New birth is often treated as interchangeable with salvation, sonship, inheritance, or completed Christian maturity.

Corrective: New birth establishes life, origin, and Kingdom capacity. It does not itself complete formation, inheritance, or maturity.

E.10 - Υἱοθεσία (*Huiothesia*)

Son-Placing and Inheritance

Lexical Range: adoption, son-placement, filial standing.

Textual Function: *Huiothesia* refers to relational status and inheritance orientation within God's household.

Common Drift: Adoption is often reduced to legal inclusion only.

Corrective: Sonship includes status, but it is not exhausted by status. In Scripture it is tied to formation, maturity, likeness, inheritance, and participation in God's purposes.

E.11 - Δικαιόω (*Dikaioō*)

To Declare Right, Vindicate, or Set Right

Lexical Range: to justify, declare righteous, vindicate, set right.

Textual Function: *Dikaioō* often functions in judicial or forensic contexts, especially in Paul, though it should not be made to carry the whole weight of salvation language by itself.

Common Drift: Justification is often treated as the totality of God's saving work.

Corrective: Justification addresses standing, verdict, and vindication. It is important, but it does not by itself encompass healing, new birth, sonship, formation, inheritance, or Kingdom participation.

E.12 - Κηρύσσω (*Kērussō*)

To Proclaim as a Herald

Lexical Range: to announce publicly, proclaim authoritatively, herald.

Textual Function: *Kērussō* describes authoritative proclamation of news.

Common Drift: Preaching is often reduced to teaching doctrines or explaining ideas.

Corrective: The gospel is not first argued as theory. It is proclaimed as news. The herald announces what has happened, what is true, and what demands Response.

E.13 - Εὐαγγέλιον (*Euangelion*)

Good News of a Reign

Lexical Range: good news, glad tidings, royal announcement.

Textual Function: In the first-century world, *euangelion* could function in royal or imperial settings as public announcement concerning rule, victory, accession, or regime.

Common Drift: Gospel is often reduced to a "plan of salvation" or a method for obtaining private assurance.

Corrective: The gospel announces a King, a Kingdom, and the consequences of His reign. Saving acts belong within that announcement, but do not replace it.

E.14 - Καλῶ (*Kaleō*)

To Call, Invite, and Summon

Lexical Range: to call, invite, summon, name, appoint.

Textual Function: God's call initiates movement, summons Response, and draws persons into participation.

Common Drift: Calling is often treated as an inward feeling only.

Corrective: In Scripture, calling is frequently active and directional. It summons a person into Response, vocation, or participation under God's purpose.

E.15 - Ἅγιος (*Hagios*)

Set Apart, Consecrated, and Purposed

Lexical Range: holy, set apart, consecrated, dedicated.

Textual Function: *Hagios* describes separation unto God's purpose. It is vocational and relational before it is merely moral.

Common Drift: Holiness is often reduced to moral flawlessness or behavioral untouchability.

Corrective: Holiness in Scripture includes moral implications, but begins with consecration and belonging to God's purpose.

Function of This Appendix

Appendix E serves as a lexical correction and stabilization tool for this book. It exists so that key gospel words are not quietly redefined by later assumptions while reading or writing.

It ensures that:

- grace is not mistaken for force
- mercy is not collapsed into grace
- faith is not reduced to mental agreement
- repentance is not reduced to emotion
- *sozo* is not collapsed into a single afterlife formula
- *sōtēria* is not reduced to destination language
- the Kingdom remains the larger context of the gospel

This appendix does not replace exegesis.

It disciplines vocabulary.

References (General)

1. BDAG, *A Greek-English Lexicon of the New Testament and Other Early Christian Literature*, 3rd ed., s.v. "χάρις."

2. BDAG, *A Greek-English Lexicon of the New Testament and Other Early Christian Literature*, 3rd ed., s.v. "σῴζω."

3. John M. G. Barclay, *Paul and the Gift* (Grand Rapids: Eerdmans, 2015).

4. Joel B. Green, *Body, Soul, and Human Life* (Grand Rapids: Baker Academic, 2008).

5. N. T. Wright, *Paul and the Faithfulness of God* (Minneapolis: Fortress Press, 2013).

6. George Eldon Ladd, *The Presence of the Future* (Grand Rapids: Eerdmans, 1974).

7. Louw & Nida, *Greek-English Lexicon of the New Testament Based on Semantic Domains.*

Appendix F

Reading Sōzō in Kingdom Context

An Interpretive Summary of Appendix A

Purpose and Function

Appendix A provides the lexical and contextual categorization of *sōzō* in the New Testament. This appendix serves a narrower purpose. It summarizes what those categories mean when read within the Gospel of the Kingdom.

The goal here is not to repeat the lexical data already presented, nor to create a second classification system. It is to state plainly what the New Testament pattern implies: *sōzō* does not announce a separate gospel. It describes what happens when the reign of God confronts what is broken, bound, threatened, disordered, or perishing.

In that sense, the saving language of the New Testament is Kingdom language.

A Necessary Clarification

Jesus did not preach a gospel of escape. He preached the Gospel of the Kingdom. The language of saving appears throughout the New Testament, but it does not stand as an independent message detached from that Kingdom. It names the concrete effects of God's reign when it enters a situation.

When the sick are made whole, *sōzō* is present. When the endangered are rescued, *sōzō* is present. When the oppressed are delivered, *sōzō* is present. When the sinner is restored, *sōzō* is present. When a people are preserved, *sōzō* is present. When the faithful are brought through to final vindication, *sōzō* is present.

The word does not carry one fixed theological content regardless of context. It takes its force from the condition the Kingdom is confronting.

Kingdom, Not a Separate Salvation System

The saving acts described by *sōzō* are not interruptions in Jesus' message. They are manifestations of it.

When Jesus healed, He was not pausing the Kingdom proclamation. He was revealing it. When He restored the broken, He was not merely illustrating the Kingdom. He was demonstrating it. The reign of God does not only promise future deliverance. It actively confronts disorder.

This is why Appendix A matters. Once the usages of *sōzō* are allowed to stand in their own contexts, the word becomes larger, more concrete, and more integrated into the Kingdom story than later reductions have often allowed.

Summary of the Pattern

Appendix A shows that *sōzō* in the New Testament includes:

- bodily healing
- rescue from immediate danger
- deliverance from oppressive domination
- restoration from the effects of sin
- preservation of persons and communities
- future vindication and eschatological deliverance

These are not unrelated meanings. They are different manifestations of the same saving reality: the reign of God confronting what threatens life.

Why This Matters

If *sōzō* is detached from the Kingdom, it is easily reduced to a private afterlife formula.

If *sōzō* is read within the Kingdom, its range becomes coherent.

It heals. It rescues. It delivers. It restores. It preserves. It vindicates.

And all of it belongs to the same gospel: the Gospel of the Kingdom.

Function of This Appendix

Appendix F is not a replacement for Appendix A. It is an interpretive control for reading Appendix A correctly.

It exists to ensure that the lexical data of *sōzō* is not abstracted from the larger theological claim of this book:

The Gospel remains the Gospel of the Kingdom.

Everything that is saved is saved because the King has come near.

Scripture Index:

- Matthew 4:17
- Matthew 12:28
- Luke 8:36
- Mark 5:34
- Luke 17:19
- Acts 2:47
- Romans 10:9–13
- 1 Thessalonians 5:9
- Hebrews 9:28
- 1 Peter 1:5

Appendix G

Sōzō and Sōtēria: Rescue, Formation, and Inheritance

Why This Appendix Exists

One of the greatest points of confusion in modern Christianity is not baptism, faith, or obedience - it is language. In particular, the English word *salvation* has been asked to carry meanings Scripture never assigned to it.

This appendix exists to restore biblical precision, not to dismantle anyone's faith.

Scripture speaks carefully. We must do the same.

Two Greek Words - One English Problem

The New Testament regularly uses two related but distinct Greek terms that English translations often flatten into one word.

sōzō (σῴζω) - verb

To rescue, heal, restore, deliver, preserve, make whole.

sōtēria (σωτηρία) - noun

Salvation/deliverance as an *outcome or state* -what "rescue" looks like when spoken of as something that arrives, is entered, is being received over time, and is ultimately unveiled.

These words are related - but they are not interchangeable. Scripture does not confuse them. Theology should not either.

sōzō - Rescue When the Kingdom Arrives

The verb **sōzō** describes what happens when God intervenes in real time.

It is:

- immediate

- situational

- restorative

- often visible in its effects

People are *saved* (sōzō) from:

- danger (Matthew 8:25)

- sickness (Mark 5:34)

- bondage (Luke 8:36)

- loss and ruin (Luke 19:9 – see note below)

sōzō is not a courtroom verdict. It is a rescue event.

It describes what happens when the Kingdom of God becomes present and active in a life. This is why Scripture can speak of people being "saved" in ways that are clearly present-tense and earthly: healed, restored, delivered, preserved:

- before the cross

- before Pentecost

- before any developed afterlife theology

They were rescued, not relocated.

Luke 19:9 - "Today Salvation Has Come to This House"

"Today salvation has come to this house, because he also is a son of Abraham."

This passage often raises concern, but the context resolves the tension.

What happened that day?

- Zacchaeus repented
- He restored what he had stolen
- He realigned his life under God's rule
- Jesus publicly affirmed that the Kingdom had entered his house

Luke uses the noun (sōtēria) - but the moment described is a Kingdom-arrival rescue in real time: a life brought back under God's reign. This was not a declaration of final inheritance. It was a present rescue and restoration.

In Luke's Gospel, *salvation coming* consistently means:

- deliverance has arrived
- authority has shifted
- a life has come back under God's reign

Zacchaeus experienced **sōzō** - rescue - not the end-of-the-age consummation.

sōtēria - Salvation Spoken in Three Movements

The New Testament speaks of sōtēria in more than one time-frame. That is not contradiction - it is how Scripture holds Kingdom reality and inheritance reality together.

1) Salvation as Present Arrival (entered now)

Sometimes salvation is spoken of as something that has come, is present, or is available now - the Kingdom arriving with rescue, restoration, and realignment.

Examples:

- "Now is the day of salvation (sōtēria)" (2 Corinthians 6:2)
- "Today salvation (sōtēria) has come to this house" (Luke 19:9)
- "My eyes have seen Your salvation (sōtērion)" (Luke 2:30)

This is salvation in the sense of God's reign breaking into a life.

2) Salvation as Ongoing Reception (already underway)

Sometimes salvation is spoken of as something being received in motion - real, present, working toward its intended end.

Example:

- "Receiving the end of your faith, the salvation (sōtēria) of your souls" (1 Peter 1:9)

This is crucial: Scripture can speak of salvation as being received, while still pointing toward "the end." Receiving does not always mean "finished." It can mean "actively being brought into."

3) Salvation as Future Unveiling (not yet fully manifested)

Sometimes salvation is framed as something nearer, ready to be revealed, or tied to Christ's appearing - language that places fullness on the horizon.

Examples:

- "Our salvation (sōtēria) is nearer now than when we first believed" (Romans 13:11)
- "A salvation (sōtēria) ready to be revealed in the last time" (1 Peter 1:5)
- "He will appear… for salvation (eis sōtērian) to those who eagerly wait for Him" (Hebrews 9:28)

This is salvation spoken of as inheritance unveiled - not merely rescue experienced.

Progressive Reality, Earnest, and Inheritance

Scripture repeatedly treats the Kingdom as something that arrives now and is lived under, while inheritance is something that is proved, formed, and finally unveiled.

The New Testament even speaks of the Spirit as an earnest / guarantee (a down payment) of what is coming (Ephesians 1:13–14; 2 Corinthians 1:22). That means the life of the Kingdom is not a static "ticket" - it is the beginning of an inheritance that must be faithfully carried.

This is why Scripture can hold these truths together without contradiction:

- rescue can be real now
- formation can be required over time
- inheritance can be unveiled later

Jesus' own teachings confirm this pattern:

- servants are judged **after** being entrusted
- branches are cut off **after** being connected
- sons can be disinherited **after** being in the house

To be *cast out*, one must first have entered. This is not instability. It is sonship.

Why Scripture Holds the Tension

The Bible intentionally holds these truths together:

- You can be rescued now and still warned later
- You can be saved today and judged tomorrow
- You can belong and still squander inheritance

Salvation is not a ticket. It is a life lived under authority.

How This Relates to Baptism

This book does not present baptism as:

- a ritual guaranteeing eternal destiny

- a substitute for faith

- a mechanical transaction

Instead, baptism consistently appears in Scripture as a Response to rescue already initiated.

- Acts 2:38 - repentance and baptism follow awakening

- Acts 22:16 - obedience follows revelation

- Acts 8, Acts 10, Acts 16, Acts 19 - water answers what God has already begun

Baptism:

- does **not** cause rescue (sōzō)

- does **not** complete inheritance (sōtēria)

- bears witness to a life turning under Kingdom authority

- positions a person on the path where inheritance is formed and proved.

Salvation Is Not the Gospel - the Kingdom Is

Jesus did not preach *salvation* as the message.

He preached:

- "The Kingdom of God is at hand"

- "Repent"

- "Follow Me"

Rescue (sōzō) is what happens when the Kingdom arrives.

Salvation as outcome (sōtēria) is what Scripture often speaks of as unfolding and finally unveiled as the Kingdom is faithfully lived under.

This is why Scripture speaks of:

- saved people who later fall away
- servants cast out
- branches removed
- sheep and goats separated

Judgment assumes participation. Inheritance assumes faithfulness.

What This Book Is - and Is Not - Saying

This book does not deny:

- faith
- grace
- the cross
- eternal inheritance
- future judgment

It does insist that:

- Scripture treats rescue (sōzō) as present and lived
- Scripture often frames salvation-as-outcome (sōtēria) as future-facing, weighty, and perseverance
- baptism belongs to sonship formation, not ritual assurance

If this distinction feels uncomfortable, it is likely because modern theology trained us to expect finality where Scripture taught formation.

For Further Study

This appendix intentionally remains concise.

A full biblical, linguistic, and theological exploration of:

- sōzō
- sōtēria
- judgment
- inheritance
- Kingdom formation

is developed in the companion volume:

Sōzō: What Am I Saved From?

These two books are designed to work together, not compete.

Appendix H References

Bauer, W., Danker, F. W., Arndt, W. F., & Gingrich, F. W. (2000). *A Greek-English lexicon of the New Testament and other early Christian literature* (3rd ed.). University of Chicago Press.

Eynikel, E., Lust, J., & Hauspie, K. (2003). *A Greek-English lexicon of the Septuagint* (Rev. ed.). Deutsche Bibelgesellschaft.

Kittel, G., & Friedrich, G. (Eds.). (1964–1976). *Theological dictionary of the New Testament* (G. W. Bromiley, Trans.; Vols. 1–10). Wm. B. Eerdmans.

Liddell, H. G., Scott, R., Jones, H. S., & McKenzie, R. (1996). *A Greek-English lexicon* (9th ed. with revised supplement). Clarendon Press.

Louw, J. P., & Nida, E. A. (1989). *Greek-English lexicon of the New Testament: Based on semantic domains* (2nd ed., Vols. 1–2). United Bible Societies.

Moulton, J. H., & Milligan, G. (1930). *The vocabulary of the Greek Testament: Illustrated from the papyri and other non-literary sources.* Hodder & Stoughton.

Mounce, W. D. (2006). *Mounce's complete expository dictionary of Old and New Testament words.* Zondervan.

Appendix H
Potholes in the Romans Road

There is a road many have been taught to walk.

It is built from selected lines in Romans. It is preached as a sequence. Admit you are a sinner. Believe Jesus died for you. Confess Him with your mouth. Call on His name. Secure heaven. Settle eternity.

But the problem is not Romans.

The problem is what has been done to Romans.

A letter written to the saints in Rome has often been reduced to a sales script for anxious sinners. Paul addressed people he called "*beloved of God*" and "*called to be saints*," and he said their faith was spoken of throughout the world (Romans 1:7–8). Romans was not first written as a tract for strangers trying to figure out how to go to heaven when they died. It was written to a believing assembly, so they would understand the righteousness of God, the work of Christ, the place of Jew and Gentile, the overthrow of sin's reign, the life of the Spirit, and the hope of glory.

That matters, because once the audience is forgotten, the whole letter gets flattened. Romans becomes a rescue pamphlet for escaping hell instead of an apostolic unveiling of what God has done in Christ to confront sin, death, flesh, condemnation, division, and corruption. The Romans Road is not always wrong because of what it says. It is often wrong because of how small it makes Paul's argument.

The first pothole is this: Romans is treated like a tract instead of a theological letter to believers. Paul is not merely teaching men how to start. He is teaching a church what has happened, what is happening, and what still will happen through Christ. That is why the letter can speak in expansive ways about salvation rather than reducing it to one moment, one prayer, or one future destination.

Consider how the usual road begins. *"All have sinned, and come short of the glory of God"* (Romans 3:23). True. Necessary. But Paul is not merely trying to make individuals feel guilty enough to repeat a prayer. He is leveling Jew and Gentile together under sin so that no flesh can boast before God. His argument is larger than private failure. Humanity as a whole has missed glory, lost right order, and come under powers it cannot master on its own. Romans 3 diagnoses the ruin, but it does not license us to reduce salvation to a minimal formula.

Then comes another famous line: *"the wages of sin is death"* (Romans 6:23). Again, true. But Romans 6 does not read like a chapter about postmortem geography. It reads like a chapter about mastery, embodiment, bondage, and freedom. Paul says believers have been united with Christ in death and resurrection (Romans

6:3–5). He says the old man was crucified (Romans 6:6). He says not to let sin reign in the mortal body (Romans 6:12). He says sin shall not have dominion (Romans 6:14). The chapter is saturated with present-life language. Death here is not smaller than final judgment, but it is certainly larger than "hell later." It is the harvest of sin's dominion breaking into life now.

That leads to one of the greatest potholes in the road: Romans 5 is often quoted, but only halfway. Many stop at *"Christ died for us"* (Romans 5:8), as though Paul's burden were merely to explain that Jesus died so people can go to heaven. But Paul does not stop at His death. He says that, having been reconciled by the death of God's Son, *"much more... we shall be saved by his life"* (Romans 5:10). That is one of the strongest blows against the shrunken version of the gospel. Paul does not present salvation as a static legal transaction only. He presents the living Christ as active in the saving work. The cross matters, but the risen Christ is not a footnote. He is central.

And around Romans 5:12–21, another error enters. Some read verse 17 - *"they which receive abundance of grace and of the gift of righteousness shall reign in life by one, Jesus Christ"* - as though Paul were speaking only of a heavenly monarchy someday (Romans 5:17). But that is not what the phrase says. Paul's contrast is with Adam's trespass, through which death reigned. Then he says those who receive grace and the gift of righteousness will reign in life. The very next movement of the letter explains this in present moral and embodied terms: do not let sin reign in your mortal body (Romans 6:12). In other words, Paul is not talking about a delayed heavenly royalty only. He is talking about a present overthrow of death's rule and sin's dominion in the life of the believer now.

This matters because the Romans Road often replaces Paul's language of dominion with destination language. Paul asks who reigns now: death, sin, flesh, or Christ? The popular system asks only where you will go later. But Paul's gospel invades the present. It breaks tyrannies. It reorders the body. It renews the mind. It makes righteousness something embodied, not merely imputed and postponed. That is why Romans 8 can speak of the Spirit giving life even to mortal bodies (Romans 8:11), of believers putting to death the deeds of the body by the Spirit (Romans 8:13), and of sons led by the Spirit of God (Romans 8:14). Paul is not writing abstractly about a far-off heaven alone. He is describing the beginning of a new reign breaking into this life.

Then there is Romans 10:9–13, perhaps the center of the modern formula. Confess with your mouth. Believe in your heart. Call on the name of the Lord. And many treat this as mechanism: say the sentence, secure the result.

But Paul is not giving a magic incantation.

Confessing "Jesus is Lord" is not a bare religious phrase. It is an allegiance claim. It means Caesar is not lord. Sin is not lord. Self is not lord. The crucified and risen Jesus is Lord. And believing God raised Him from the dead is not merely agreeing that a miracle happened. It is trusting that God has vindicated and enthroned the rejected Son (Romans 10:9–10).

Even *"whosoever shall call upon the name of the Lord shall be saved"* must be read in that light (Romans 10:13). Paul is quoting Joel 2:32, where the calling is tied to deliverance under the intervention of God. The background is not a modern altar call. It is covenantal rescue. That does not make Romans 10 smaller. It makes it larger. The one who calls on the Lord is not merely reciting a line to obtain an afterlife policy. He is appealing to the Lord who alone delivers.

And the word translated "saved" there deserves more care than it usually receives. The Greek verb is *sozo*. Lexically it can carry the sense of save, rescue, preserve, heal, or make whole. That does not mean Romans 10:13 should be treated as a blank check for every possible form of rescue in the same way or to the same degree. Context still governs emphasis. In Romans 10, the foreground is the Lord's rescuing deliverance to those who call upon Him in faith and confession under His lordship. But the breadth of the word means we have no right to shrink Paul's promise into mere destination language. The verse presents not only a promise of real deliverance, but a pattern: the Lord is the One who rescues those who call upon Him.

This is where the broader distinction matters. Romans does not only use the verb *sozo*. It also uses the noun *soteria* (Romans 1:16; 10:10; 11:11; 13:11). And that noun often carries the broader salvation-horizon of God's purpose rather than one isolated rescue-act. The problem with the Romans Road is not simply that it mishandles one verse. It is that it often collapses *sozo* and *soteria* into one thin idea and then forces every saving text in Romans to serve that narrowed reading.

Another pothole appears when Romans is treated as though salvation were exhausted in one past moment. Paul simply does not speak that way. In Romans 8:24 he says, *"we are saved by hope,"* and immediately connects salvation to what is not yet seen and still awaited. Then in Romans 13:11 he tells believers, *"now is our salvation nearer than when we believed."* Those are not the words of a man who thinks salvation can be collapsed into one instant and then discussed only as a completed ticket to heaven. Paul speaks of salvation as already entered and still approaching in fuller manifestation.

So the real problem with the Romans Road is not always that it lies. It is that it miniaturizes. It turns a letter about the righteousness of God, the reign of grace, the collapse of sin's dominion, the life of the Spirit, the hope of resurrection, and the future liberation of creation into a transaction outline. It often gives men a way to feel safe without demanding that the rule of death be broken in their present lives.

But Romans does not allow that reduction.

Romans announces that death reigned through Adam, but grace reigns through righteousness through Jesus Christ (Romans

5:21). Romans announces not merely forgiveness, but transfer of dominion. Romans announces not merely acquittal, but union. Romans announces not merely that Christ died, but that the reconciled are saved by His life (Romans 5:10). Romans announces not merely that sinners need mercy, but that saints must understand what kind of salvation they have entered and what kind of reign has begun.

A better reading of Romans, then, does not ask only, "How do I get to heaven?" It asks, "What has Christ come to save me from?" Romans answers: from wrath (Romans 5:9), from enmity (Romans 5:10), from the reign of death (Romans 5:17), from the dominion of sin (Romans 6:14), from condemnation (Romans 8:1), from the futility of the flesh (Romans 8:5–13), and ultimately from corruption itself (Romans 8:21–23).

That is why Romans fits far better with a *sozo* framework than with the reduced formula commonly preached in its name. Salvation in Romans is judicial, relational, transformational, bodily, and future-facing all at once. It begins now, invades now, and reaches toward resurrection fullness.

So the potholes in the Romans Road are not minor cracks in the pavement. They are signs that the road was made too narrow for the terrain Paul was crossing.

He was not writing a script to help sinners secure a heavenly address.

He was unveiling the reign of God in Christ against the reign of sin and death.

He was not offering a prayer formula.

He was proclaiming a Lord.

He was not shrinking salvation to what happens after burial.

He was showing what begins when death loses its crown.

And that is why Romans must not be used to preach a gospel smaller than the one Paul actually wrote.

Because the Christ of Romans does not merely prepare men for another world.

He begins to take them back from this one.

Scripture Index:

- Romans 1:7–8
- Romans 1:16
- Romans 3:23
- Romans 5:8
- Romans 5:9
- Romans 5:10
- Romans 5:17
- Romans 5:21
- Romans 6:3–6
- Romans 6:12
- Romans 6:14
- Romans 6:23
- Romans 8:1
- Romans 8:5–14
- Romans 8:11
- Romans 8:13
- Romans 8:21–24
- Romans 10:9–10
- Romans 10:13
- Romans 11:11

- Romans 13:11
- Joel 2:32

Glossary of Terms

Adoption (Huiothesia). Son-placement. Not merely emotional inclusion, but being placed in family standing with inheritance in view.

Baptism. The obedient, public, bodily Response to the Kingdom announcement. In this book baptism is neither a bare symbol nor a magic rite; it is a real act of cleansing, burial, transition, and incorporation under Christ.

Basileia (Kingdom). Active reign or rule. Kingdom language in Scripture speaks first of authority being exercised, not merely of a location.

Belief / Faith (Pistis / Pisteuo). Trust, allegiance, and reliance upon Jesus the King. More than mental agreement, it is entrusting oneself to His word.

Body of Christ. The people of God as one living body under one Head. The book stresses that God's saving work is corporate as well as personal.

Born Again / From Above. Language from John 3 that points to new life sourced from above. The emphasis is divine origin, not merely repetition.

Born of Water and Spirit. Jesus' language for Kingdom entry. In this book it marks the beginning of Kingdom life, not the completion of the whole journey.

Communion. Participation in the body and blood of Christ, not mere ritual memory. It calls the church to shared life, shared discernment, and shared order.

Deliverance. Rescue from oppressive spiritual power, bondage, or domination. A form of sozo when God breaks what holds a person captive.

Discern the Body. To recognize the body of Christ rightly in shared life and at the Lord's Table. In 1 Corinthians, failure here has real bodily and communal consequences.

Eleos (Mercy). Compassion that withholds deserved judgment and meets misery with pity. Mercy is related to grace but not identical to it.

Euangelion (Gospel). Good news. In this book the gospel is chiefly the announcement that God's reign has drawn near in Christ.

Firstborn. Christ as the preeminent Son and heir. He is the pattern and head of the many sons God is bringing to glory.

Forensic. A courtroom or judicial way of speaking. The book argues that some passages use legal categories, but not every saving text should be forced into that frame.

Formation. The Father's training of sons for maturity, likeness, and readiness. Not self-improvement, but family preparation.

Fruit of the Spirit. The character the Spirit forms within God's people: love, joy, peace, and the rest. Fruit governs how gifts should function.

Gifts of the Spirit. Distributed manifestations of the Spirit for the common good. In the book they are treated as saving acts expressed through the Body.

Grace (Charis). God's favorable initiative, gift, and welcome. Grace is not an impersonal force that replaces obedience; it creates the ground on which obedience becomes possible.

Healing. A saving act in which God restores the body or embodied life. Many New Testament uses of sozo clearly carry this sense.

Inheritance. What is prepared for sons and heirs in Christ. In the book, inheritance is tied to maturity, resurrection, shared reign, and responsibility.

Justification (Dikaioo). To declare righteous, vindicate, or set right in judicial terms. Important, but not the only way the New Testament speaks of God's saving work.

Kingdom of God. God's active reign breaking into the present and moving toward final fullness.

Kingdom of Heaven. Matthew's reverential way of speaking about the same Kingdom reality, not a second kingdom.

Metanoia (Repentance). A turning of mind, direction, and allegiance in Response to the King. More than regret, it is reorientation.

New Birth. The generation of life from above. It grants Kingdom capacity, but it is not identical with every act of rescue or the full inheritance of sons.

Reconciliation. Restoration of broken relationship. In Romans 5 it describes peace with God secured through Christ, but Paul continues on toward life, reign, and glory.

Remission of Sins. Release or sending away of sins. The book distinguishes remission from healing, sonship, and inheritance so that each biblical category can speak with its own weight.

Reign in Life. Paul's language in Romans 5 for the overthrow of death's rule under Christ. The phrase is treated here as present-life Kingdom language, not merely future-heaven language.

Rescue. A plain English way of describing what sozo often does. God intervenes where life is threatened.

Restoration. Return to wholeness, right order, right relation, or rightful place.

Salvation Horizon. A summary phrase used in the manuscript for the larger scope of God's saving purpose beyond one isolated rescue moment.

Saving Act. A repeated phrase in the book for an actual intervention of God against what threatens life - healing, rescue, deliverance, preservation, or restoration.

Sonship. Family identity, likeness, and inheritance-position in
Christ. The book presents sonship, not rescue alone, as the
larger aim of Christ's work.

Spirit as Earnest. The Holy Spirit as pledge, down payment, or
foretaste of inheritance. His present work previews what is
still to come.

Soteria. The broader salvation horizon or outcome of God's
saving work. The New Testament can speak of it as
present, being received, or still to be revealed.

Sozo. To save, heal, restore, deliver, preserve, or make whole. In
this book it usually refers to a concrete saving act in
context.

Wholeness. Life restored under God's reign - body, soul,
relationships, and vocation brought back toward right
order.

Witness of Works. Jesus' works do not merely help people; they
testify that the Father sent Him and that the Kingdom has
drawn near.

Thematic Word Index

Scripture Index

Other Good Books
from EKI Publishing

www.ekibooks.com

- ***The Unique Factor***
  - By David Webb

- ***Escape the Shame of Babylon***
  - By David Webb

- ***Building the Kingdom Through the Local Church***
  - By David Webb

- ***Building the Temple to Hold the Glory***
  - By David Webb

- ***Unchained: Freed to be His Treasure***
  - By Kirkland M. Rite

- ***Baptized: Why did I get Wet***
  - By Kirland M. Rite

- ***Sozo: What Am I Saved From?***
  - By Kirland M. Rite

- ***Covenant of Salt: The Gospel and a Pretzel***
  - By Kirland M. Rite

Coming from Eternal Kingdom International Publishing

2026

Covenant of Salt

By Kirkland M. Rite

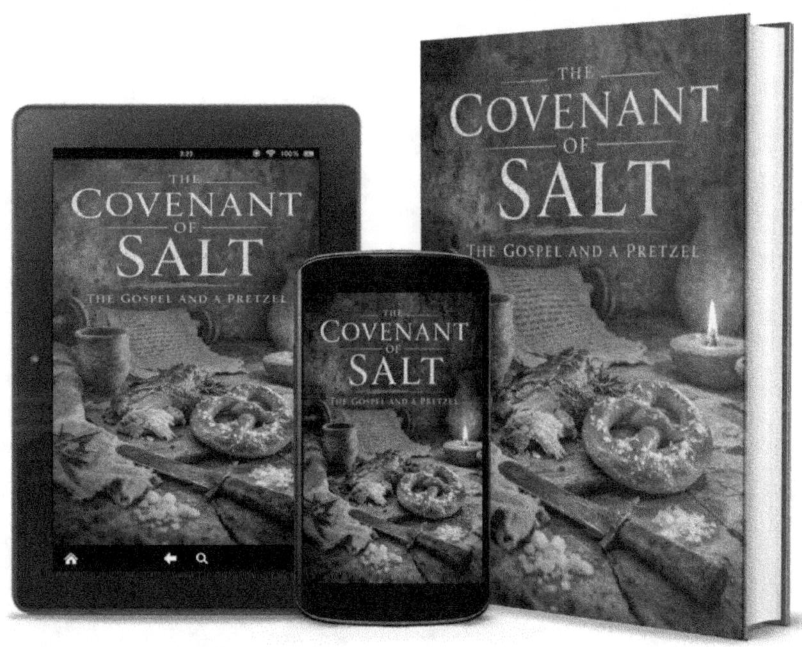